PENGUIN BOOKS

Walks in

1. *Voices of Akenfield* Ronald Blythe
2. *The Wood* John Stewart Collis
3. *From Dover to the Wen* William Cobbett
4. *The Pleasures of English Food* Alan Davidson
5. *Through England on a Side-Saddle* Celia Fiennes
6. *Elegy Written in a Country Churchyard and Other Poems* Various
7. *A Shropshire Lad* A. E. Housman
8. *Cathedrals and Castles* Henry James
9. *Walks in the Wheat-fields* Richard Jefferies
10. *The Beauties of a Cottage Garden* Gertrude Jekyll
11. *Country Churches* Simon Jenkins
12. *A Wiltshire Diary* Francis Kilvert
13. *Some Country Houses and their Owners* James Lees-Milne
14. *The Clouded Mirror* L. T. C. Rolt
15. *Let Us Now Praise Famous Gardens* Vita Sackville-West
16. *One Green Field* Edward Thomas
17. *English Folk Songs* Ralph Vaughan Williams and A. L. Lloyd
18. *Country Lore and Legends* Jennifer Westwood and Jacqueline Simpson
19. *Birds of Selborne* Gilbert White
20. *Life at Grasmere* Dorothy and William Wordsworth

WALKS IN
THE
WHEAT-FIELDS

Richard
Jefferies

English Journeys

PENGUIN BOOKS

Published by the Penguin Group
Penguin Books Ltd, 80 Strand, London WC2R ORL, England
Penguin Group (USA) Inc., 375 Hudson Street, New York, New York 10014, USA
Penguin Group (Canada), 90 Eglinton Avenue East, Suite 700, Toronto, Ontario, Canada M4P 2Y3
(a division of Pearson Penguin Canada Inc.)
Penguin Ireland, 25 St Stephen's Green, Dublin 2, Ireland
(a division of Penguin Books Ltd)
Penguin Group (Australia), 250 Camberwell Road, Camberwell, Victoria 3124, Australia
(a division of Pearson Australia Group Pty Ltd)
Penguin Books India Pvt Ltd, 11 Community Centre, Panchsheel Park, New Delhi – 110 017, India
Penguin Group (NZ), 67 Apollo Drive, Rosedale, North Shore 0632, New Zealand
(a division of Pearson New Zealand Ltd)
Penguin Books (South Africa) (Pty) Ltd, 24 Sturdee Avenue, Rosebank, Johannesburg 2196, South Africa

Penguin Books Ltd, Registered Offices: 80 Strand, London WC2R ORL, England

www.penguin.com

These extracts taken from *Wild Life in a Southern County*, first published 1879, *The Amateur Poacher*, first
published 1879 and *Field and Hedgerow*, first published 1889
Published in Penguin Books 2009

3

All rights reserved

Set by Rowland Phototypesetting Ltd, Bury St Edmunds, Suffolk
Printed in England by Clays Ltd, St Ives plc

ISBN: 978-0-141-19099-0

www.greenpenguin.co.uk

Penguin Books is committed to a sustainable future
for our business, our readers and our planet.
The book in your hands is made from paper
certified by the Forest Stewardship Council.

A Note on the Text

'Rooks Returning to Roost' taken from *Wild Life in a Southern County* (1879); 'The First Gun', 'Woodland Twilight', 'Farmer Willum's Place' and 'Ferreting' all taken from *The Amateur Poacher* (1879) and 'Walks in the Wheat-fields' taken from *Field and Hedgerow* (1889).

Contents

1. Rooks Returning to Roost

As evening approaches, and the rooks begin to wing their way homewards, sometimes a great number of them will alight upon the steep ascent close under the entrenchment on the downs which has been described, and from whence the wood and beech trees where they sleep can be seen. They do not seem so much in search of food, of which probably there is not a great deal to be found in the short, dried-up herbage and hard soil, as to rest here, half-way home from arable fields. Sometimes they wheel and circle in fantastic flight over the very brow of the down, just above the rampart; occasionally, in the raw cold days of winter, they perch moping in disconsolate mood upon the bare branches of the clumps of trees on the ridge.

After the nesting time is over and they have got back to their old habits – which during that period are quite reversed – it is a sight to see from hence the long black stream in the air steadily flowing onwards to the wood below. They stretch from here to the roosting-trees, fully a mile and a half – literally as the crow flies; and backwards in the opposite direction the line reaches as far as the eye can see. It is safe to estimate that the aerial army's line of march extends over quite five miles in one unbroken corps. The breadth they occupy in the atmosphere varies – now twenty yards, now fifty, now a hundred, on an average say fifty yards; but rooks do not fly very close together like starlings, and the mass, it may be observed, fly on the same plane. Instead of three or four layers one above the other, the greater number pass by at the same height from the ground, side by side on a level, as soldiers would march upon a road: not meaning, of course, an absolute, but a relative level. This formation is more apparent from an elevation – as it were, up among them – than from below; and looking along their line towards the distant wood it is like glancing under a black canopy.

Small outlying parties straggle from the line – now on one side, now on the other; sometimes a few descend to alight on trees in the meadows, where doubtless their nests were situated in the spring. For it is a habit of theirs, months after the nesting is over and also before it begins, to pay a flying visit to the trees in the evening, calling *en route* to see that all is well and to assert possession.

The rustling sound of these thousands upon thousands of wings beating the air with slow steady stroke can hardly be compared to anything else in its weird oppressiveness, so to say: it is a little like falling water, but may be best likened, perhaps, to a vast invisible broom sweeping the sky. Every now and then a rook passes with ragged wing – several feathers gone, so that you can see daylight through it; sometimes the feathers are missing from the centre, leaving a great gap, so that it looks as if the bird had a large wing on this side and on the other two narrow ones. There is a rough resemblance between these and the torn sails of some of the old windmills which have become dark in colour from long exposure to the weather, and have been rent by the storms of years. Rooks can fly with gaps of astonishing size in their wings, and do not seem much incommoded by the loss – caused, doubtless, by a charge of shot in the rook-shooting, or by the small sharp splinters of flint with which the birdkeepers sometimes load their guns, not being allowed to use shot.

Near their nesting-trees their black feathers may be picked up by dozens in the grass; they beat them out occasionally against the small boughs, and sometimes in fighting. If seen from behind, the wings of the rook, as he spreads them and glides, slowly descending, preparatory to alighting, slightly turn up at the edges like the rim of a hat, but much less curved. From a distance as he flies he appears to preserve a level course, neither rising nor falling; but if observed nearer it will be seen that with every stroke of the wings the body is lifted some inches, and sinks as much immediately afterwards.

As the black multitude floats past overhead with deliberate, easy flight, their trumpeters and buglemen, the jackdaws – two or three to every company – utter their curious chuckle; for the jackdaw is a bird which could not keep silence to save his life, but must talk after his fashion, while his grave, solemn companions move slowly onwards, rarely deigning to 'caw' him a reply. But away yonder at the wood, above the great beech trees, where so vast a congregation is gathered together, there is a mighty uproar and commotion: a seething and bubbling of the crowds, now settling on the branches, now rising in sable clouds, each calling to the other with all his might, the whole population delivering its opinions at once.

It is an assemblage of a hundred republics. We know how free States indulge in speech with their parliaments and congresses and senates, their public meetings, and so forth: here are a hundred such nations, all with perfect liberty of tongue holding forth unsparingly, and in a language which consists of two or three syllables indefinitely repeated. The din is wonderful – each republic as its forces arrive adding to the noise, and for a long time unable to settle upon their trees, but feeling compelled to wheel around and discourse. In spring each tribe has its special district, its own canton and city, in its own trees away in the meadows. Later on they all meet here in the evening. It is a full hour or more before the orations have all been delivered, and even then small bands rush up into the air still dissatisfied.

This great stream of rooks passing over the hills meets another great stream as it approaches the wood, crossing up from the meadows. From the rampart there may be seen, perhaps a mile and a half away, a dim black line crossing at right angles – converging on the wood, which itself stands on the edge of the table-land from which the steeper downs arise. This second army is every whit as numerous, as lengthy, and as regular in its route as the first.

Every morning, from the beech trees where they have slept, safe at that elevation from all the dangers of the night, there set out these two vast expeditionary corps. Regularly the one flies steadily eastward over the downs; as regularly the other flies steadily northwards over the vale and meadows. Doubtless in different country districts their habits in this respect vary; but here it is always east and always north. If any leave the wood for the south or the west, as probably they do, they go in small bodies and are quickly lost sight of. The two main divisions sail towards the sunrise and towards the north star.

They preserve their ranks for at least two miles from the wood; and then gradually first one and then another company falls out, and wheeling round, descends upon some favourite field, till by degrees, spreading out like a fan, the army melts away. In the evening the various companies, which may by that time have worked far to the right or to the left, gradually move into line. By-and-by the vanguard comes sweeping up, and each regiment rises from the meadow or the hill, and takes its accustomed place in the return journey.

So that although if you casually observe a flock of rooks in the daytime they seem to wander hither and thither just as fancy leads, or as they are driven by passers-by, in reality they have all their special haunts; they adhere to certain rules, and even act in concert, thousands upon thousands of them at once, as if in obedience to the word of command, and as if aware of the precise moment at which to move. They have their laws, from which there is no deviation: they are handed down unaltered from generation to generation. Tradition, indeed, seems to be their main guide, as it is with savage human tribes. They have their particular feeding grounds; and so you may notice that, comparing ten or a dozen fields, one or two will almost always be found to be frequented by rooks while the rest are vacant.

Here, for instance, is a meadow close to a farmstead – what is usually called the home-field, from its proximity to a house – here day after day rooks alight and spend hours in it, as much at their ease as the nag or the lambs brought up by hand. Another field, at a distance, which to the human eye appears so much more suitable, being retired, quiet, and apparently quite as full of food, is deserted; they scarcely come near it. The home-field itself is not the attraction, because other home-fields are not so favoured.

The tenacity with which rooks cling to localities is often illustrated near great cities where buildings have gradually closed in around their favourite haunts. Yet on the small waste spots covered with cinders and dust-heaps, barren and unlovely, the rooks still alight: and you may see them, when driven up from such places, perching on the telegraph wires over the very steam of the locomotives as they puff into the station.

I think that neither considerations of food, water, shelter, nor convenience, are always the determining factors in the choice made by birds of the spots they frequent; for I have seen many cases in which all of these were evidently quite put on one side. Birds to ordinary observation seem so unfettered, to live so entirely without rhyme or reason, that it is difficult to convey the idea that the precise contrary is really the case.

Returning to these two great streams of rooks, which pour every evening in converging currents from the north and east upon the wood; why do they do this? Why not go forth to the west, or to the south, where there are hills and meadows and streams in equal number? Why not scatter abroad, and return according to individual caprice? Why, to go still further, do rooks manoeuvre in such immense numbers, and crows fly only in pairs? The simple truth is that birds, like men, have a history. They are unconscious of it, but its accomplished facts affect them still and shape the course of their existence. Without doubt, if we could trace that history back there are good and sufficient reasons why rooks prefer to fly in this particular locality, to the east and to the north. Something may perhaps be learnt by examining the routes along which they fly.

The second division – that which goes northwards, after flying little more than a mile in a straight line – passes over Wick Farm, and disperses gradually in the meadows surrounding and extending far below it. The rooks whose nests are placed in the elms of the Warren belong to this division, and, as their trees are the nearest to the great central roosting-place, they are the first to quit the line of march in the morning, descending to feed in the fields around their property. On the other hand, in the evening, as the army streams homewards, they are the last to rise and join the returning host.

So that there are often rooks in and about the Warren later in the evening after those whose habitations are farther away have gone by, for, having so short a distance to fly, they put off the movement till the last moment. Before watches became so common a possession, the labouring people used, they say, to note the passage overhead of the rooks in the morning in winter as one of their signs of time, so regular was their appearance;

and if the fog hid them, the noise from a thousand black wings and throats could not be missed.

If, from the rising ground beyond the Warren or from the downs beyond that, the glance is allowed to travel slowly over the vale northwards, instead of the innumerable meadows which are really there, it will appear to consist of one vast forest. Of the hamlet not far distant there is nothing visible but the white wall of a cottage, perhaps, shining in the sun, or the pale blue smoke curling upwards. This wooded appearance is caused by timber trees standing in the hedgerows, in the copses at the corners of the meadows, and by groups and detached trees in the middle of the fields.

Many hedges are full of elms, some have rows of oaks; some meadows have trees growing so thickly in all four hedges as to seem surrounded by a timber wall; one or two have a number of ancient spreading oaks dotted about in the field itself, or standing in rows. But there are not nearly so many trees as there used to be. Numerous hedges have been grubbed to make the fields larger.

Within the last thirty years two large falls of timber have taken place, when the elms especially were thrown wholesale. The old men, however, recall a much greater 'throw', as they term it, of timber, which occurred twice as long ago. Then before that they have a tradition that a still earlier 'throw' took place, when the timber chiefly went to the dockyards for the building of those wooden walls which held the world at bay. These traditions go back, therefore, some eighty or a hundred years. One field in particular is pointed out where stood a double row or avenue of great oaks leading to nothing but a farmstead of the ordinary sort, of which there is not the slightest record that it ever was anything but a farmhouse. Now avenues of great oaks are not planted to lead to farmsteads. Besides these, it is said, there were oaks in most of the fields – oaks that have long since disappeared, the prevalent tree being elm.

While all these 'throws' of timber have successively taken place, no attempt has been made to fill up the gaps; no planting of acorns, no shielding with rails the young saplings from the ravages of cattle. If a young tree could struggle up it could; if not, it perished. At the last two 'throws', especially, young trees which ought to have been saved were ruthlessly cut down. Yet even now the place is well timbered; so that it is easy to form some idea of the forest-like appearance it must have presented a hundred years ago, when rows of giant oaks led up to that farmhouse door.

Then there are archaeological reasons, which it would be out of place to mention, why in very ancient days a forest, in all probability, stood hereabouts. It seems reasonable to suppose that in one way or another the regular flight of the second army of rooks passing down into this district was originally attracted by the trees. Three suggestions arise out of the circumstances.

The wood in which both streams of rooks roost at night stands on the last slope of the downs; behind it to the south extend the hills, and the open tilled upland plains; below it northwards are the meadows. It has, therefore, much the appearance of the last surviving remnant of the ancient forest. There has been a wood there time out of mind: there are references to the woods of the locality dating from the sixteenth century. Now if we suppose (and such seems to have been really the case) the unenclosed woodlands below gradually cleared of trees – thereby doubtless destroying many rookeries – the rooks driven away would naturally take refuge in the wood remaining. There the enclosure protected them, and there the trees, being seldom or never cut down, or if cut down felled with judgment and with a view to future timber, grew to great size and in such large groups as they prefer. But as birds are creatures of habit, their descendants in the fiftieth generation would still revisit the old places in the meadows.

Secondly, although so many successive 'throws' of timber thinned out the trees, yet there may still be found more groups and rows of elms and oak in this direction than in any other; that is, a line drawn northwards from the remaining wood passes through a belt of well-timbered country. On either side of this belt there is much less timber; so that the rooks that desired to build nests beyond the limits of the enclosed wood still found in the old places the best trees for their purpose. Here may be seen far more rookeries than in any other direction. Hardly a farmhouse lying near this belt but has got its rookery, large or small. Once these rookeries were established, an inducement to follow this route would arise in the invariable habit of the birds of visiting their nesting-trees even when the actual nesting time is past.

Thirdly, if the inquiry be carried still farther back, it is possible that the line taken by the rooks indicates the line of the first clearings in very early days. The clearing away of trees and underwood, by opening the ground and rendering it accessible, must be very attractive to birds, and rooks are particularly fond of following the plough. Now although the district is at present chiefly meadow land, numbers of these meadows were originally ploughed fields, of which there is evidence in the surface of the fields themselves, where the regular 'lands' and furrows are distinctly visible.

One or all of these suggestions may perhaps account for the course followed by the rooks. In any case it seems natural to look for the reason in the trees. The same idea applies to the other stream of rooks which leaves the wood for the eastward every morning, flying along the downs. In describing the hill district, evidence was given of the existence of woods or forest land upon the downs in the olden time. Detached copses and small woods are still to be found; and it happens that a part of this district, in the line of the eastward flight, belonged to a 'chase' of which several written notices are extant.

The habits of rooks seem more regular in winter than in summer. In winter the flocks going out in the morning or returning in the evening appear to pass nearly at the same hour day after day. But in summer they often stay about late. This last summer I noticed a whole flock, some hundreds in number, remaining out till late – till quite dusk – night after night, and always in the same place. It was an arable field, and there they stood close together on the ground, so close that in spots it was difficult to distinguish individuals. They were silent and still, making no apparent attempt at feeding. The only motion I observed was when a few birds arrived and alighted among them. Where they thus crowded together the earth was literally black.

It was about three-quarters of a mile from their nesting-trees, but nesting had been over for more than two months. This particular field had recently been ploughed by steam tackle, and was the only one for a considerable distance that had been ploughed for some time. There they stood motionless, side by side, as if roosting on the ground; possibly certain beetles were numerous just there (for it was noticeable that they chose the same part of the field evening after evening), and came crawling up out of the earth at night.

The jackdaws which – so soon as the rooks pack after nesting and fly in large flocks – are always with them, may be distinguished by their smaller size and the quicker beats of their wings, even when not uttering their well-known cry. Jackdaws will visit the hencoops if not close to the house, and help themselves to the food meant for the fowls. Poultry are often kept in rickyards, a field or two distant from the homestead, and it is then amusing to watch the impudent attempts of the jackdaws at robbery. Four or five will perch on the post and rails, intent on the tempting morsels: sitting with their heads a little on one side and peering over. Suddenly one thinks he sees an opportunity. Down he hops, and takes a peck, but before he has hardly seized it, a hen darts across, running at him with beak extended like lance in rest. Instantly he is up on the rail again, and the impetus of the hen's charge carries her right under him.

Then, while her back is turned, down hops a second and helps himself freely. Out rushes another hen, and up goes the jackdaw. A pause ensues for a few minutes: presently a third black rascal dashes right into the midst of the fowls, picks up a morsel, and rises again before they can attack him. The way in which the jackdaw dodges the hens though alighting among them, and as it were for the moment surrounded, is very clever: and it is laughable to see the cool impudence with which he perches again on the rail, and looks down demurely, not a whit abashed, on the feathered housewife he has just been doing his best to rob.

2. *The First Gun*

They burned the old gun that used to stand in the dark corner up in the garret, close to the stuffed fox that always grinned so fiercely. Perhaps the reason why he seemed in such a ghastly rage was that he did not come by his death fairly. Otherwise his pelt would not have been so perfect. And why else was he put away up there out of sight? – and so magnificent a brush as he had too. But there he stood, and mounted guard over the old flintlock that was so powerful a magnet to us in those days. Though to go up there alone was no slight trial of moral courage after listening to the horrible tales of the carters in the stable, or the old women who used to sit under the hedge in the shade, on an armful of hay, munching their crusts at luncheon time.

The great cavernous place was full of shadows in the brightest summer day; for the light came only through the chinks in the shutters. These were flush with the floor and bolted firmly. The silence was intense, it being so near the roof and so far away from the inhabited parts of the house. Yet there were sometimes strange acoustical effects – as when there came a low tapping at the shutters, enough to make your heart stand still. There was then nothing for it but to dash through the doorway into the empty cheese-room adjoining, which was better lighted. No doubt it was nothing but the labourers knocking the stakes in for the railing round the rickyard, but why did it sound just exactly outside the shutters? When that ceased the staircase creaked, or the pear-tree boughs rustled against the window. The staircase always waited till you had forgotten all about it before the loose worm-eaten planks sprang back to their place.

Had it not been for the merry whistling of the starlings on the thatch above, it would not have been possible to face the gloom and the teeth of Reynard, ever in the act to snap, and the mystic noises, and the sense of guilt – for the gun was forbidden. Besides which there was the black mouth of the open trapdoor overhead yawning fearfully – a standing terror and temptation; for there was a legend of a pair of pistols thrown up there out of the way – a treasure-trove tempting enough to make us face anything. But Orion must have the credit of the courage; I call him Orion because he was a hunter and had a famous dog. The last I heard of him he had just ridden through a prairie fire, and says the people out there think nothing of it.

We dragged an ancient linen-press under the trapdoor, and put some boxes on that, and finally a straight-backed oaken chair. One or two of those chairs were split up and helped to do the roasting on the kitchen hearth. So, climbing the pile, we emerged under the rafters, and could see daylight faintly in several places coming through the starlings' holes. One or two bats fluttered to and fro as we groped among the lumber, but no pistols could be discovered; nothing but a cannon-ball, rusty enough and about as big as an orange, which they say was found in the wood, where there was a brush in Oliver's time.

In the middle of our expedition there came the well-known whistle, echoing about the chimneys, with which it was the custom to recall us to dinner. How else could you make people hear who might be cutting a knobbed stick in the copse half a mile away or bathing in the lake? We had to jump down with a run; and then came the difficulty; for black dusty cobwebs, the growth of fifty years, clothed us from head to foot. There was no brushing or picking them off, with that loud whistle repeated every two minutes.

The fact where we had been was patent to all; and so the chairs got burned – but one, which was rickety. After which a story crept out, of a disjointed skeleton lying in a corner under the thatch. Though just a little suspicious that this might be a *ruse* to frighten us from a second attempt, we yet could not deny the possibility of its being true. Sometimes in the dusk, when I sat poring over 'Koenigsmark, the Robber', by the little window in the cheese-room, a skull seemed to peer down the trapdoor. But then I had the flintlock by me for protection.

There were giants in the days when that gun was made; for surely no modern mortal could have held that mass of metal steady to his shoulder. The linen-press and a chest on the top of it formed, however, a very good gun-carriage; and, thus mounted, aim could be taken out of the window at the old mare feeding in the meadow below by the brook, and a 'bead' could be drawn upon Molly, the dairymaid, kissing the fogger behind the hedge, little dreaming that the deadly tube was levelled at them. At least this practice and drill had one useful effect – the eye got accustomed to the flash from the pan, instead of blinking the discharge, which ruins the shooting. Almost everybody and everything on the place got shot dead in this way without knowing it.

It was not so easy as might be supposed to find proper flints. The best time to look for them was after a heavy storm of rain had washed a shallow channel beside the road, when you might select some hardy splinters which had lain hidden under the dust. How we were found out is not quite clear: perhaps the powder left a smell of sulphur for any one who chanced to go up in the garret.

But, however that may be, one day, as we came in unexpectedly from a voyage in the punt, something was discovered burning among the logs on the kitchen hearth; and, though a desperate rescue was attempted, nothing was left but the barrel of our precious gun and some crooked iron representing the remains of the lock. There are things that are never entirely forgotten, though the impression may become fainter as years go by. The sense of the cruel injustice of that act will never quite depart.

But they could not burn the barrel, and we almost succeeded in fitting it to a stock of elder. Elder has a thick pith running down the centre: by removing that the gouge and chisel had not much work to do to make a groove for the old bell-mouthed barrel to lie in. The matchlock, for as such it was intended, was nearly finished when our hopes were dashed to the ground by a piece of unnatural cunning. One morning the breech-piece that screwed in was missing. This was fatal. A barrel without a breechpiece is like a cup without a bottom. It was all over.

There are days in spring when the white clouds go swiftly past, with occasional breaks of bright sunshine lighting up a spot in the landscape. That is like the memory of one's youth. There is a long dull blank, and then a brilliant streak of recollection. Doubtless it was a year or two afterwards when, seeing that the natural instinct could not be suppressed but had better be recognised, they produced a real gun (single-barrel) for me from the clock-case.

It stood on the landing just at the bottom of the dark flight that led to the garret. An oaken case six feet high or more, and a vast dial, with a mysterious picture of a full moon and a ship in full sail that somehow indicated the quarters of the year, if you had been imitating Rip Van Winkle and after a sleep of six months wanted to know whether it was spring or autumn. But only to think that all the while we were puzzling over the moon and the ship and the queer signs on the dial a gun was hidden inside! The case was locked, it is true; but there are ways of opening locks, and we were always handy with tools.

This gun was almost, but not quite so long as the other. That dated from the time between Stuart and Hanover; this might not have been more than seventy years old. And a beautiful piece of workmanship it was: my new double breechloader is a coarse common thing to compare with it. Long and slender and light as a feather, it came to the shoulder with wonderful ease. Then there was a groove on the barrel at the breech and for some inches up which caught the eye and guided the glance like a trough to the sight at the muzzle and thence to the bird. The stock was shod with brass, and the trigger-guard was of brass, with a kind of flange stretching half-way down to the butt and inserted in the wood. After a few minutes' polishing it shone like gold, and to see the sunlight flash on it was a joy.

You might note the grain of the barrel, for it had not been browned; and it took a good deal of sand to get the rust off. By aid of a little oil and careful wiping after a shower it was easy to keep it bright. Those browned barrels only encourage idleness. The lock was a trifle dull at first, simply from lack of use. A small screwdriver soon had it to pieces, and it speedily clicked again sweet as a flute. If the hammer came back rather far when at full-cock, that was because the lock had been converted from a flint, and you could not expect it to be absolutely perfect. Besides which, as the fall was longer the blow was heavier, and the cap was sure to explode.

By old farmhouses, mostly in exposed places (for which there is a reason), one or more huge walnut trees may be found. The provident folk of those days planted them with the purpose of having their own gunstocks cut out of the wood when the tree was thrown. They could then be sure it was really walnut, and a choice piece of timber thoroughly well seasoned. I like to think of those times, when men settled themselves down, and planted and planned and laid out their gardens and orchards and woods, as if they and their sons and sons' sons, to the twentieth generation, were sure to enjoy the fruit of their labour.

The reason why the walnuts are put in exposed places, on the slope of a rise, with open aspect to the east and north, is because the walnut is a foolish tree that will not learn by experience. If it feels the warmth of a few genial days in early spring, it immediately protrudes its buds; and the next morning a bitter frost cuts down every hope of fruit for that year, leaving the leaf as black as may be. Wherefore the east wind is desirable to keep it as backward as possible.

There was a story that the stock of this gun had been cut out of a walnut tree that was thrown on the place by my great-grandfather, who saw it well seasoned, being a connoisseur of timber, which is, indeed, a sort of instinct in all his descendants. And a vast store of philosophy there is in timber if you study it aright.

After cleaning the gun and trying it at a mark, the next thing was to get a good shot with it. Now there was an elm that stood out from the hedge a little, almost at the top of the meadow, not above five-and-twenty yards from the other hedge that bounded the field. Two mounds could therefore be commanded by any one in ambush behind the elm, and all the angular corner of the mead was within range.

It was not far from the house; but the ground sank into a depression there, and the ridge of it behind shut out everything except just the roof of the tallest hayrick. As one sat on the sward behind the elm, with the back turned on the rick and nothing in front but the tall elms and the oaks in the other hedge, it was quite easy to fancy it the verge of the prairie with the backwoods close by.

The rabbits had scratched the yellow sand right out
into the grass – it is always very much brighter in colour
where they have just been at work – and the fern, already
almost yellow too, shaded the mouths of their buries.
Thick bramble bushes grew out from the mound and
filled the space between it and the elm: there were a few
late flowers on them still, but the rest were hardening
into red sour berries. Westwards, the afternoon sun,
with all his autumn heat, shone full against the hedge
and into the recess, and there was not the shadow of a
leaf for shelter on that side.

The gun was on the turf, and the little hoppers kept
jumping out of the grass on to the stock: once their king,
a grasshopper, alighted on it and rested, his green limbs
tipped with red rising above his back. About the distant
wood and the hills there was a soft faint haze, which is
what Nature finishes her pictures with. Something in
the atmosphere which made it almost visible: all the
trees seemed to stand in a liquid light – the sunbeams
were suspended in the air instead of passing through.
The butterflies even were very idle in the slumberous
warmth; and the great green dragon-fly rested on a leaf,
his tail arched a little downwards, just as he puts it when
he wishes to stop suddenly in his flight.

The broad glittering trigger-guard got quite hot in the
sun, and the stock was warm when I felt it every now
and then. The grain of the walnut-wood showed plainly
through the light polish: it was not varnished like the
stock of the double-barrel they kept padlocked to the
rack over the high mantelpiece indoors. Still you could
see the varnish. It was of a rich dark horse-chestnut

colour, and yet so bright and clear that if held close you could see your face in it. Behind it the grain of the wood was just perceptible; especially at the grip, where hard hands had worn it away somewhat. The secret of that varnish is lost – like that of the varnish on the priceless old violins.

But you could feel the wood more in my gun: so that it was difficult to keep the hand off it, though the rabbits would not come out; and the shadowless recess grew like a furnace, for it focussed the rays of the sun. The heat on the sunny side of a thick hedge between three and four in the afternoon is almost tropical if you remain still, because the air is motionless: the only relief is to hold your hat loose; or tilt it against your head, the other edge of the brim on the ground. Then the grass-blades rise up level with the forehead. There is a delicious smell in growing grass, and a sweetness comes up from the earth.

Still it got hotter and hotter; and it was not possible to move in the least degree, lest a brown creature sitting on the sand at the mouth of his hole, and hidden himself by the fern, should immediately note it. And Orion was waiting in the rickyard for the sound of the report, and very likely the shepherd too. We knew that men in Africa, watched by lions, had kept still in the sunshine till, reflected from the rock, it literally scorched them, not daring to move; and we knew all about the stoicism of the Red Indians. But Ulysses was ever my pattern and model: that man of infinite patience and resource.

So, though the sun might burn and the air become suffocating in that close corner, and the quivering line of heat across the meadow make the eyes dizzy to watch, yet not a limb must be moved. The black flies came in crowds; but they are not so tormenting if you plunge your face in the grass, though they titillate the back of the hand as they run over it. Under the bramble bush was a bury that did not look much used; and once or twice a great blue fly came out of it, the buzz at first sounding hollow and afar off and becoming clearer as it approached the mouth of the hole. There was the carcass of a dead rabbit inside no doubt.

A humble-bee wandering along – they are restless things – buzzed right under my hat, and became entangled in the grass by my ear. Now we knew by experience in taking their honey that they could sting sharply if irritated, though good-tempered by nature. How he 'burred' and buzzed and droned! – till by-and-by, crawling up the back of my head, he found an open space and sailed away. Then, looking out again, there was a pair of ears in the grass not ten yards distant: a rabbit had come out at last. But the first delight was quickly over: the ears were short and sharply pointed, and almost pinkly transparent.

What would the shepherd say if I brought home one of his hated enemies no bigger than a rat? The young rabbit made waiting still more painful, being far enough from the hedge to get a clear view into the recess if anything attracted his notice. Why the shepherd hated rabbits was because the sheep would not feed where they had worn their runs in the grass. Not the least movement was possible now – not even that little shifting which makes a position just endurable: the heat seemed to increase; the thought of Ulysses could hardly restrain the almost irresistible desire to stir.

When, suddenly, there was a slight rustling among the boughs of an oak in the other hedge, as of wings against twigs: it was a woodpigeon, better game than a rabbit. He would, I knew, first look round before he settled himself to preen his feathers on the branch, and, if everything was still while that keen inspection lasted, would never notice me. This is their habit – and the closer you are underneath them the less chance of their perceiving you: for a pigeon perched rarely looks straight downwards. If flying, it is just the reverse; for then they seem to see under them quicker than in any other direction.

Slowly lifting the long barrel of the gun – it was fortunate the sunlight glancing on the bright barrel was not reflected towards the oak – I got it to bear upon the bird; but then came a doubt. It was all eight-and-twenty yards across the angle of the meadow to the oak – a tremendous long shot under the circumstances. For they would not trust us with the large copper powder-flask, but only with a little pistol-flask (it had belonged to the pair of pistols we tried to find), and we were ordered not to use more than a charge and a half at a time. That was quite enough to kill blackbirds. (The noise of the report was always a check in this way; such a trifle of powder only made a slight puff.)

Shot there was in plenty – a whole tobacco-pipe bowl full, carefully measured out of the old yellow canvas money-bag that did for a shot belt. A starling could be knocked off the chimney with this charge easily, and so could a blackbird roosting in a bush at night. But a wood-pigeon nearly thirty yards distant was another matter; for the old folk (and the birdkeepers too) said that their quills were so hard the shot would glance aside unless it came with great force. Very likely the pigeon would escape, and all the rabbits in the buries would be too frightened to come out at all.

A beautiful bird he was on the bough, perched well in view and clearly defined against the sky behind; and my eye travelled along the groove on the breech and up the barrel, and so to the sight and across to him; and the finger, which always would keep time with the eye, pulled at the trigger.

A mere puff of a report, and then a desperate fluttering in the tree and a cloud of white feathers floating above the hedge, and a heavy fall among the bushes. He was down, and Orion's spaniel (that came racing like mad from the rickyard the instant he heard the discharge) had him in a moment. Orion followed quickly. Then the shepherd came up, rather stiff on his legs from rheumatism, and stepped the distance, declaring it was thirty yards good; after which we all walked home in triumph.

Molly the dairymaid came a little way from the rick-yard, and said she would pluck the pigeon that very night after work. She was always ready to do anything for us boys; and we could never quite make out why they scolded her so for an idle hussy indoors. It seemed so unjust. Looking back, I recollect she had very beautiful brown eyes.

'You mind you chaws the shot well, measter,' said the shepherd, 'afore you loads th' gun. The more you chaws it the better it sticks the-gither, an' the furder it kills um;' a theory of gunnery that which was devoutly believed in in his time and long anticipated the wire cartridges. And the old soldiers that used to come round to hay-making, glad of a job to supplement their pensions, were very positive that if you bit the bullet and indented it with your teeth, it was perfectly fatal, no matter to what part of the body its billet took it.

In the midst of this talk as we moved on, I carrying the gun at the trail with the muzzle downwards, the old ramrod, long disused and shrunken, slipped half out; the end caught the ground, and it snapped short off in a second. A terrible disaster this, turning everything to bitterness: Orion was especially wroth, for it was his right next to shoot. However, we went down to the smithy at the inn, to take counsel of the blacksmith, a man of knowledge and a trusty friend. 'Aha!' said he, 'it's not the first time I've made a ramrod. There's a piece of lancewood in the store overhead which I keep on purpose; it's as tough as a bow – they make carriage-shafts of it; you shall have a better rod than was ever fitted to a Joe Manton.' So we took him down some pippins, and he set to work on it that evening.

3. Woodland Twilight:
Traitors on the Gibbet

In a hedge that joined a wood, and about a hundred yards from it, there was a pleasant hiding-place beside a pollard ash. The bank was hollow with rabbit-buries: the summer heat had hardened the clay of the mound and caused it to crack and crumble wherever their excavations left a precipitous edge. Some way up the trunk of the tree an immense flat fungus projected, roughly resembling the protruding lip of a savage enlarged by the insertion of a piece of wood. It formed a black ledge standing out seven or eight inches, two or three inches thick, and extending for a foot or more round the bark. The pollard, indeed, was dead inside, and near the ground the black touch-wood showed. Ash timber must become rarer year by year: for, being so useful, it is constantly cut down, while few new saplings are planted or encouraged to become trees.

In front a tangled mass of bramble arched over the dry ditch; it was possible to see some distance down the bank, for nothing grew on the top itself, the bushes all rising from either side – a peculiarity of clay mounds. This narrow space was a favourite promenade of the rabbits; they usually came out there for a few minutes first, looking about before venturing forth into the meadows. Except a little moss, scarcely any vegetation other than underwood clothed the bare hard soil of the mound; and for this reason every tiny aperture that suited their purpose was occupied by wasps.

They much prefer a clear space about the entrance to their nests, affording an unencumbered passage: there were two nests within a few yards of the ash. Though so generally dreaded, wasps are really inoffensive insects, never attacking unless previously buffeted. You may sit close to a wasps' nest for hours, and, if you keep still, receive no injury. Humble-bees, too, congregate in special localities: along one hedge half a dozen nests may be found, while other fields are searched for them in vain.

The best time to enter such a hiding-place is a little before the sun sinks: for as his beams turn red all the creatures that rest during the day begin to stir. Then the hares start down from the uplands and appear on the short stubble, where the level rays throw exaggerated shadows behind them. When six or eight hares are thus seen near the centre of a single field, they and their shadows seem to take possession of and occupy it.

Pheasants, though they retire to roost on the trees, often before rising come forth into the meadows adjacent to the coverts. The sward in front of the pollard ash sloped upwards gradually to the foot of a low hill planted with firs, and just outside these about half a dozen pheasants regularly appeared in the early evening. As the sun sank below the hill, and the shadow of the great beeches some distance away began to extend into the mead, they went back one by one into the firs. There they were nearly safe, for no trees give so much difficulty to the poacher. It is not easy even to shoot anything inside a fir plantation at night: as for the noose, it is almost impossible to use it. The lowest pheasant is taken first, and then the next above, like fowls perched on the rungs of a ladder; and, indeed, it is not unlikely that those who excel in this kind of work base their operations upon previous experiences in the hen roost.

The wood pigeons begin to come home, and the wood is filled with their hollow notes: now here, now yonder, for as one ceases another takes it up. They cannot settle for some time: each as he arrives perches awhile, and then rises and tries a fresh place, so that there is a constant clattering. The green woodpecker approaches at a rapid pace – now opening, now closing his wings, and seeming to throw himself forward rather than to fly. He rushes at the trees in the hedge as though he could pierce the thick branches like a bullet. Other birds rise over or pass at the side: he goes through, arrow-like, avoiding the boughs. Instead of at once entering the wood, he stays awhile on the sward of the mead in the open.

As the pheasants generally feed in a straight line along the ground, so the lesser pied woodpecker travels across the fields from tree to tree, rarely staying on more than one branch in each, but, after examining it, leaves all that may be on other boughs and seeks another ahead. He rises round and round the dead branch in the elm, tapping it with blows that succeed each other with marvellous rapidity. He taps for the purpose of sounding the wood to see if it be hollow or bored by grubs, and to startle the insects and make them run out for his convenience. He will ascend dead branches barely half an inch thick that vibrate as he springs from them, and proceeds down the hedge towards the wood. The 'snop-top' sounds in every elm, and grows fainter as he recedes. The sound is often heard, but in the thick foliage of summer the bird escapes unseen, unless you are sitting almost under the tree when he arrives in it.

Then the rooks come drifting slowly to the beeches: they are uncertain in their hour at this season – some, indeed, scarce care to return at all; and even when quite dusk and the faint stars of summer rather show themselves than shine, twos and threes come occasionally through the gloom. A pair of doves pass swiftly, flying for the lower wood, where the ashpoles grow. The grasshoppers sing in the grass, and will continue till the dew descends. As the little bats flutter swiftly to and fro just without the hedge, the faint sound of their wings is audible as they turn: their membranes are not so silent as feathers, and they agitate them with extreme velocity. Beetles go by with a loud hum, rising from those isolated bunches of grass that may be seen in every field; for the cows will not eat the rank green blades that grow over and hide dried dung.

A large white spot, ill-defined and shapeless in the distance and the dimness, glides along the edge of the wood, then across in front before the fir plantation, next down the hedge to the left, and presently passes within two yards, going towards the wood again along this mound. It is a white owl: he flies about five feet from the ground and absolutely without a sound. So when you are walking at night it is quite startling to have one come overhead, approaching from behind and suddenly appearing. This owl is almost fearless; unless purposely alarmed he will scarcely notice you, and not at all if you are still.

As he reaches the wood he leaves the hedge, having gone all round the field, and crosses to a small detached circular fir plantation in the centre. There he goes out of sight a minute or two; but presently appears skirting the low shed and rickyard yonder, and is finally lost behind the hedges. This round he will go every evening, and almost exactly at the same time – that is, in reference to the sun, which is the clock of nature.

Step never so quietly out from the mound, the small birds that unnoticed have come to roost in the bushes will hear it and fly off in alarm. The rabbits that are near the hedge rush in; those that are far from home crouch in the furrows and the bunches. Crossing the open field, they suddenly start as it seems from under your feet – one white tail goes dapping up and down this way, another jerks over the 'lands' that way. The moonbeams now glisten on the double-barrel; and a bright sparkle glitters here and there as a dewdrop catches a ray.

Upon the grass a faint halo appears; it is a narrow band of light encircling the path, an oval ring – perhaps rather horseshoe shape than oval. It glides in front, keeping ever at the same distance as you walk, as if there the eye was focussed. This is only seen when the grass is wet with dew, and better in short grass than long. Where it shines the grass looks a paler green. Passing gently along a hedge thickly timbered with oak and elms, a hawk may perhaps start forth: hawks sometimes linger by the hedges till late, but it is not often that you can shoot one at roost except in spring. Then they invariably return to roost in the nest tree, and are watched there, and so shot, a gunner approaching on each side of the hedge. In the lane dark objects – rabbits – hasten away, and presently the footpath crosses the still motionless brook near where it flows into the mere.

The low brick parapet of the bridge is overgrown with mosses; great hedges grow each side, and the willows, long uncut, almost meet in the centre. In one hedge an opening leads to a drinking-place for cattle: peering noiselessly over the parapet between the boughs, the coots and moorhens may be seen there feeding by the shore. They have come up from the mere as the ducks and teal do in the winter. The broader waters can scarcely be netted without a boat, but the brook here is the very place for a moonlight haul. The net is stretched first across the widest spot nearest to the pool, that no fish may escape. They swim up here in the daytime in shoals, perch especially; but the night poachers are often disappointed, for the fish seem to retire to deeper waters as the darkness comes on. A black mass of mud-coated sticks, rotten twigs, and thorn bushes, entangled in the meshes, is often the only result of much toil.

Once now and then, as when a preserved pond is netted, a tremendous take occurs; but nets are rather gone by, being so unwieldy and requiring several men to manage effectually. If they are not hung out to dry properly after being used, they soon rot. Now, a large net stretched along railings or a hedge is rather a conspicuous object, and brings suspicion on the owner. It is also so heavy after use that until wrung, which takes time, a strong man can barely carry it; and if a sudden alarm comes it must be abandoned.

It is pleasant to rest awhile on the parapet in the shadow of the bushes. The low thud-thud of sculls in the rowlocks of a distant punt travels up the water. By-and-by a hare comes along, enters on the bridge, and almost reaches the gate in the middle before he spies anything suspicious. Such a spot, and, indeed, any gateway, used to be a favourite place to set a net, and then drive the hares towards it with a cur dog that ran silent. Bold must be the man that would set a net in a footpath now, with almost every field preserved by owner or tenant. With a bound the hare hies back and across the meadow: the gun comes to the shoulder as swiftly.

On the grass lit by the moon the hare looked quite distinct, but the moment the gaze is concentrated up the barrel he becomes a dim object with no defined outline. In shooting on the ground by twilight or in the moon-beams, waste no time in endeavouring to aim, but think of the hare's ears – say a couple of feet in front of his tail – and the moment the gun feels steady pull the trigger. The flash and report come together; there is a dull indescribable sound ahead, as some of the shot strikes home in fur and some drills into the turf, and then a rustling in the grass. The moorhens dive, and the coots scuttle down the brook towards the mere at the flash. While yet the sulphurous smoke lingers, slow to disperse, over the cool dewy sward, there comes back an echo from the wood behind, then another from the mere, then another and another beyond.

The distant sculls have ceased to work in the rowlocks

– those in the punt are listening to the echoes; most likely they have been fishing for tench in the deep holes under the black shadow of the aspens. (Tench feed in the dark: if you wish to take a big one wait till it is necessary to fix a piece of white paper on the float.) Now put the empty cartridge in your pocket instead of throwing it aside; pull the hare's neck across your knee, and hurry off. But you may safely stay to harle him; for those very echoes that have been heard a mile round about are the best safeguard: not one man in a thousand could tell the true direction whence the sound of the explosion originated.

The pleasure of wandering in a wood was so great that it could never be resisted, and did not solely arise from the instinct of shooting. Many expeditions were made without a gun, or any implement of destruction, simply to enjoy the trees and thickets. There was one large wood very carefully preserved, and so situate in an open country as not to be easily entered. But a little observation showed that the keeper had a 'habit'. He used to come out across the wheatfields to a small wayside 'public', and his route passed by a lonely barn and rickyard. One warm summer day I saw him come as usual to the 'public', and while he was there quietly slipped as far as the barn and hid in it.

In July such a rickyard is very hot; heat radiates from every straw. The ground itself is dry and hard, each crevice choked with particles of white chaff; so that even the couch can hardly grow except close under the low hedge where the pink flower of the pimpernel opens to the sky. White stone staddles – short conical pillars with broad capitals – stand awaiting the load of sheaves that will shortly press on them. Every now and then a rustling in the heaps of straw indicates the presence of mice. From straw and stone and bare earth heat seems to rise up. The glare of the sunlight pours from above. The black pitched wooden walls of the barn and sheds prevent the circulation of air. There are no trees for shadow – nothing but a few elder bushes, which are crowded at intervals of a few minutes with sparrows rushing with a whirr of wings up from the standing corn.

But the high pitched roof of the barn and of the lesser sheds has a beauty of its own – the minute vegetation that has covered the tiles having changed the original dull red to an orange hue. From ridge to eaves, from end to end, it is a wide expanse of colour, only varying so much in shade as to save it from monotony. It stands out glowing, distinct against the deep blue of the sky. The 'cheep' of fledgeling sparrows comes from the crevices above; but swallows do not frequent solitary buildings so much as those by dwelling-houses, being especially fond of cattle-sheds where cows are milked.

The proximity of animals apparently attracts them: perhaps in the more exposed places there may be dangers from birds of prey. As for the sparrows, they are innumerable. Some are marked with white patches – a few so much so as to make quite a show when they fly. One handsome cock bird has a white ring half round his neck, and his wings are a beautiful partridge-brown. He looks larger than the common sort; and there are several more here that likewise appear to exceed in size, and to have the same peculiar brown.

After a while there came the sound of footsteps and a low but cheerful whistle. The keeper having slaked a thirst very natural on such a sultry day returned, and re-entered the wood. I had decided that it would be the best plan to follow in his rear, because then there would be little chance of crossing his course haphazard, and the dogs would not sniff any strange footsteps, since the footsteps would not be there till they had gone by. To hide from the eyes of a man is comparatively easy; but a dog will detect an unwonted presence in the thickest bush, and run in and set up a yelping, especially if it is a puppy.

It was not more than forty yards from the barn to the wood: there was no mound or hedge, but a narrow, deep, and dry watercourse, a surface drain, ran across. Stooping a little and taking off my hat, I walked in this, so that the wheat each side rose above me and gave a perfect shelter. This precaution was necessary, because on the right there rose a steep Down, from whose summit the level wheat-fields could be easily surveyed. So near was it that I could distinguish the tracks of the hares worn in the short grass. But if you take off your hat no one can distinguish you in a wheat-field, more particularly if your hair is light: nor even in a hedge.

Where the drain or furrow entered the wood was a wire-netting firmly fixed, and over it tall pitched palings, sharp at the top. The wood was enclosed with a thick hawthorn hedge that looked impassable; but the keeper's footsteps, treading down the hedge-parsley and brushing aside the 'gicks', guided me behind a bush where was a very convenient gap. These signs and the smooth-worn bark of an ash against which it was needful to push proved that this quiet path was used somewhat frequently.

Inside the wood the grass and the bluebell leaves – the bloom past and ripening to seed – so hung over the trail that it was difficult to follow. It wound about the ash stoles in the most circuitous manner – now to avoid the thistles, now a bramble thicket, or a hollow filled with nettles. Then the ash poles were clothed with the glory of the woodbine – one mass of white and yellow wax-like flowers to a height of eight or nine feet, and forming a curtain of bloom from branch to branch.

After awhile I became aware that the trail was approaching the hill. At the foot it branched; and the question arose whether to follow the fork that zig-zagged up among the thickets or that which seemed to plunge into the recesses beneath. I had never been in this wood before – the time was selected because it was probable that the keeper would be extremely occupied with his pheasant chicks. Though the earth was so hard in the exposed rick-yard, here the clayey ground was still moist under the shadow of the leaves. Examining the path more closely, I easily distinguished the impression of the keeper's boot: the iron toe-plate had left an almost perfect impression, and there were the deep grooves formed by the claws of his dog as it had scrambled up the declivity and the pad slipped on the clay.

As he had taken the upward path, no doubt it led direct to the pheasants, which was sure to be on the hill itself, or a dry and healthy slope. I therefore took the other trail, since I must otherwise have overtaken him;

for he would stay long among his chicks: just as an old-fashioned farmer lingers at a gate, gazing on his sheep. Advancing along the lower path, after some fifteen minutes it turned sharply to the right, and I stood under the precipitous cliff-like edge of the hill in a narrow coombe. The earth at the top hung over the verge, and beech-trees stood as it seemed in the act to topple, their exposed roots twisting to and fro before they re-entered the face of the precipice. Large masses of chalky rubble had actually fallen, and others were all but detached. The coombe, of course, could be overlooked from thence; but a moment's reflection convinced me there was no risk, for who would dare to go near enough to the edge to look down?

The coombe was full of fir-trees; and by them stood a long narrow shed – the roof ruinous, but the plank walls intact. It had originally been erected in a field, since planted for covers. This long shed, a greenish grey from age and mouldering wood, became a place of much interest. Along the back there were three rows of weasels and stoats nailed through the head or neck to the planks. There had been a hundred in each row – about three hundred altogether. The lapse of time had entirely dissipated the substance of many on the upper row; nothing remained but the grim and rusty nail. Further along there hung small strips without shape. Beyond these the nails supported something that had a rough outline still of the animal. In the second row the dried and shrivelled creatures were closely wrapped in nature's mummy-cloth of green; in the third, some of those last exposed still retained a dull brown colour. None were recent.

Above, under the eaves, the spiders' webs had thickly gathered; beneath, the nettles flourished.

But the end of the shed was the place where the more distinguished offenders were gibbeted. A footpath, well worn and evidently much used, went by this end, and, as I afterwards ascertained, communicated with the mansion above and the keeper's cottage some distance below. Every passenger between must pass the gallows where the show of more noble traitors gave proof of the keeper's loyal activity. Four shorter rows rose in tiers. To the nails at the top strong beaks and black feathers adhered, much bedraggled and ruffled by weather. These crows had long been dead; the keeper when he shot a crow did not trouble to have it carried home, unless a nail was conspicuously vacant. The ignoble bird was left where he fell.

On the next row the black and white of magpies and the blue of jays alternated. Many of the magpies had been despoiled of their tails, and some of their wings, the feathers being saleable. The jays were more numerous, and untouched; they were slain in such numbers that the market for their plumage was glutted. Though the bodies were shrunken, the feathers were in fair condition. Magpies' nests are so large that in winter, when the leaves are off the trees, they cannot but be seen, and, the spot being marked, in the summer old and young are easily destroyed. Hawks filled the third row. The kestrels were the most numerous, but there were many sparrow-hawks. These made a great show, and were stuck so closely that a feather could hardly be thrust between them. In the midst, quite smothered under their larger wings, were the remains of a smaller bird – probably a merlin. But the last and lowest row, that was also nearest, or on a level with the face of a person looking at the gallows, was the most striking.

This grand tier was crowded with owls – not arranged in any order, but haphazard, causing a fine mixture of colour. Clearly this gallery was constantly renewed. The white owl gave the prevalent tint, side by side with the brown wood owls, and scattered among the rest, a few long horned owls – a mingling of white, yellowish brown, and tawny feathers. Though numerous here, yet trap and gun have so reduced the wood owls that you may listen half the night by a cover and never hear the 'Who-hoo' that seems to demand your name.

The barn owls are more liable to be shot, because they are more conspicuous; but, on the other hand, as they often breed and reside away from covers, they seem to escape. For months past one of these has sailed by my window every evening uttering a hissing 'skir-r-r'. Here, some were nailed with their backs to the wall, that they might not hide their guilty faces.

The delicate texture of the owl's feathers is very remarkable: these birds remind me of a huge moth. The owls were more showy than the hawks, though it is commonly said that without sunlight there is no colour – as in the case of plants grown in darkness. Yet the hawks are day birds, while the owls fly by night. There came the sound of footsteps; and I retreated, casting one glance backward at the black and white, the blue and brown colours that streaked the wall, while the dull green weasels were in perpetual shadow. By night the bats would flit round and about that gloomy place. It would not do to return by the same path, lest another keeper might be coming up it; so I stepped into the wood itself. To those who walk only in the roads, hawks and owls seem almost rare. But a wood is a place to which they all flock; and any wanderer from the north or west naturally tends thither. This wood is of large extent; but even to the smaller plantations of the Downs it is wonderful what a number come in the course of a year. Besides the shed just visited, there would be certain to be another more or less ornamented near the keeper's cottage, and probably others scattered about, where the commoner vermin could be nailed without the trouble of carrying them far away. Only the owls and hawks, magpies, and such more striking evidences of slaughter were collected here, and almost daily renewed.

To get into the wood was much easier than to get out, on account of the thick hedge, palings, and high sharp-sparred gates; but I found a dry ditch where it was possible to creep under the bushes into a meadow where was a footpath.

4. *Farmer Willum's Place: Snipe Shooting*

One October morning towards the end of the month, Orion and I started to beat over Redcote Farm upon the standing invitation of the occupier. There was a certainty of sport of some kind, because the place had remained almost unchanged for the last century. It is 'improvement' that drives away game and necessitates the pheasant preserve.

The low whitewashed walls of the house were of a dull yellowish hue from the beating of the weather. They supported a vast breadth of thatched roof drilled by sparrows and starlings. Under the eaves the swallows' nests adhered, and projecting shelves were fixed to prevent any inconvenience from them. Some of the narrow windows were still darkened with the black boarding put up in the days of the window tax.

In the courtyard a number of stout forked stakes were used for putting the dairy buckets on, after being cleaned, to dry. No attempt was made to separate the business from the inner life of the house. Here in front these oaken buckets, scoured till nearly white, their iron handles polished like silver, were close under the eyes of any one looking out. By the front door a besom leaned against the wall that every comer might clean the mud from his boots; and you stepped at once from the threshold into the sitting-room. A lane led past the garden, if that could be called a lane which widened into a field and after rain was flooded so deeply as to be impassable to foot passengers.

The morning we had chosen was fine; and after shaking hands with old Farmer 'Willum', whose shooting days were over, we entered the lane, and by it the fields. The meadows were small, enclosed with double-mounds, and thickly timbered, so that as the ground was level you could not see beyond the field in which you stood, and upon looking over the gate might surprise a flock of pigeons, a covey of partridges, or a rabbit out feeding. Though the tinted leaves were fast falling, the hedges were still full of plants and vegetation that prevented seeing through them. The 'kuck-kuck' of the redwings came from the bushes – the first note of approaching winter – and the tips of the rushes were dead. Red haws on the hawthorn and hips on the briar sprinkled the hedge with bright spots of colour.

The two spaniels went with such an eager rush into a thick double-mound, dashing heedlessly through the nettles and under the brambles, that we hastened to get one on each side of the hedge. A rustling – a short bark; another, then a movement among the rushes in the ditch, evidently not made by the dogs; then a silence. But the dogs come back, and as they give tongue the rabbit rushes past a bare spot on the slope of the bank. I fire – a snap shot – and cut out some fur, but do no further harm; the pellets bury themselves in the earth. But, startled and perhaps just stung by a stray shot, the rabbit bolts fairly at last twenty yards in front of Orion, the spaniel tearing at his heels.

Up goes the double-barrel with a bright gleam as the sunlight glances on it. A second of suspense: then from the black muzzle darts a cylinder of tawny flame and an opening cone of white smoke: a sharp report rings on the ear. The rabbit rolls over and over, and is dead before the dog can seize him. After harling the rabbit, Orion hangs him high on a projecting branch, so that the man who is following us at a distance may easily find the game. He is a labourer, and we object to have him with us, as we know he would be certain to get in the way.

We then tried a corner where two of these large mounds, meeting, formed a small copse in which grew a quantity of withy and the thick grasses that always border the stoles. A hare bolted almost directly the dogs went in: hares trust in their speed, rabbits in doubling for cover. I fired right and left, and missed: fairly missed with both barrels. Orion jumped upon the mound from the other side, and from that elevation sent a third cartridge after her.

It was a long, a very long shot, but the hare perceptibly winced. Still, she drew easily away from the dogs, going straight for a distant gateway. But before it was reached the pace slackened; she made ineffectual attempts to double as the slow spaniels overtook her, but her strength was ebbing, and they quickly ran in. Reloading, and in none of the best of tempers, I followed the mound. The miss was of course the gun's fault – it was foul; or the cartridges, or the bad quality of the powder.

We passed the well-remembered hollow ash pollard, whence, years before, we had taken the young owls, and in which we had hidden the old single-barrel gun one

44

sultry afternoon when it suddenly came on to thunder. The flashes were so vivid and the discharges seemingly so near that we became afraid to hold the gun, knowing that metal attracted electricity. So it was put in the hollow tree out of the wet, and with it the powder-flask, while we crouched under an adjacent hawthorn till the storm ceased.

Then by the much-patched and heavy gate where I shot my first snipe, that rose out of the little stream and went straight up over the top bar. The emotion, for it was more than excitement, of that moment will never pass from memory. It was the bird of all others that I longed to kill, and certainly to a lad the most difficult. Day after day I went down into the water-meadows; first thinking over the problem of the snipe's peculiar twisting flight. At one time I determined that I would control the almost irresistible desire to fire till the bird had completed his burst of zig-zag and settled to something like a straight line. At another I as firmly resolved to shoot the moment the snipe rose before he could begin to twist. But some unforeseen circumstance always interfered with the execution of these resolutions.

Now the snipe got up unexpectedly right under foot; now one rose thirty yards ahead; now he towered straight up, forced to do so by the tall willows; and occasionally four or five rising together and calling 'sceap, sceap' in as many different directions, made me hesitate at which to aim. The continual dwelling upon the problem rendered me nervous, so that I scarcely knew when I pulled the trigger.

But one day, in passing this gateway, which was a

long distance from the particular water-meadows where I had practised, and not thinking of snipes, suddenly one got up, and with a loud 'sceap' darted over the gate. The long slender gun – the old single-barrel – came to the shoulder instinctively, without premeditation, and the snipe fell.

Coming now to the brook, which was broad and bordered by a hedge on the opposite side, I held Orion's gun while he leaped over. The bank was steep and awkward, but he had planned his leap so as to alight just where he could at once grasp an ash branch and so save himself from falling back into the water. He could not, however, stay suspended there, but had to scramble over the hedge, and then called for his gun. I leaned mine against a hollow withy pollard, and called 'ready'.

Taking his gun a few inches above the trigger guard (and with the guard towards his side), holding it lightly just where it seemed to balance in a perpendicular position, I gave it a slow heave rather than a throw, and it rose into the air. This peculiar *feeling* hoist, as it were, caused it to retain the perpendicular position as it passed over brook and hedge in a low curve. As it descended it did indeed slope a little, and Orion caught it with one hand easily. The hedge being low he could see it coming; but guns are sometimes heaved in this way over hedges that have not been cropped for years. Then the gun suddenly appears in the air, perhaps fifteen feet high, while the catch depends not only upon the dexterity of the hand but the ear – to judge correctly where the person who throws it is standing, as he is invisible.

The spaniels plunged in the brook among the flags,

but though they made a great splashing nothing came of it till we approached a marshy place where was a pond. A moorhen then rose and scuttled down the brook, her legs dragging along the surface some distance before she could get up, and the sunshine sparkling on the water that dropped from her. I fired and knocked her over: at the sound of the discharge a bird rose from the low mound by the pond some forty yards ahead. My second barrel was empty in an instant.

Both Orions followed; but the distance, the intervening pollard willows, or our excitement spoilt the aim. The woodcock flew off untouched, and made straight away from the territories we could beat into those that were jealously guarded by a certain keeper with whom Farmer 'Willum' had waged war for years. 'Come on!' shouted Orion as soon as he had marked the cock down in a mound two fields away. Throwing him my gun, I leaped the brook; and we at first raced, but on second thoughts walked slowly, for the mound. Running disturbs accuracy of fire, and a woodcock was much too rare a visitor for the slightest chance to be lost.

As we approached we considered that very probably the cock would either lie close till we had walked past, and get up behind, or he would rise out of gunshot. What we were afraid of was his making for the preserves, which were not far off. So we tossed for the best position, and I lost. I had therefore to get over on the side of the hedge towards the preserves and to walk down somewhat faster than Orion, who was to keep (on his side) about thirty yards behind. The object was to flush the cock on his side, so that if missed the bird might return towards our territories. In a double-mound like this it is impossible to tell what a woodcock will do, but this was the best thing we could think of.

About half-way down the hedge I heard Orion fire both barrels in quick succession – the mound was so thick I could not see through. The next instant the cock came over the top of the hedge just above my head. Startled at seeing me so close, he flew straight down along the summit of the bushes – a splendid chance to look at from a distance; but in throwing up the gun a projecting briar caught the barrels, and before I could recover it the bird came down at the side of the hedge.

It was another magnificent chance; but again three pollard willows interfered, and as I fired the bark flew off one of them in small strips. Quickened by the whistling pellets, the cock suddenly lifted himself again to the top of the hedge to go over, and for a moment came full in view, and quite fifty yards away. I fired a snap shot as a forlorn hope, and lost sight of him; but the next instant I heard Orion call, 'He's down!' One single chance pellet had dropped the cock – he fell on the other side just under the hedge.

We hastened back to the brook, thinking that the shooting would attract the keepers, and did not stay to look at the bird till safe over the water. The long beak, the plumage that seems painted almost in the exact tints of the dead brown leaves he loves so well, the eyes large by comparison and so curiously placed towards the poll of the head as if to see behind him – there was not a point that did not receive its share of admiration. We shot about half a dozen rabbits, two more hares, and a woodpigeon afterwards; but all these were nothing compared with the woodcock.

How Farmer 'Willum' chuckled over it – especially to think that we had cut out the game from the very batteries of the enemy! It was the one speck of bitterness in the old man's character – his hatred of this keeper. Disabled himself by age and rheumatism from walking far, he heard daily reports from his men of this fellow coming over the boundary to shoot, or drive pheasant or partridge away. It was a sight to see Farmer 'Willum' stretch his bulky length in his old armchair, right before the middle of the great fire of logs on the hearth, twiddling his huge thumbs, and every now and then indulging in a hearty laugh, followed by a sip at the 'straight-cup'.

There was a stag's horn over the staircase: 'Willum' loved to tell how it came there. One severe winter long since, the deer in the forest many miles away broke cover, forced by hunger, and came into the rickyards and even the gardens. Most of them were got back, but one or two wandered beyond trace. Those who had guns were naturally on the look-out; indeed, a regular hunt was got up – 'Willum', then young and active, in it of course. This chase was not successful; but early one morning, going to look for wild geese in the water-meadow with his long-barrelled gun, he saw something in a lonely rickyard. Creeping cautiously up, he rested the heavy gun on an ash stole, and the big duck-shot tore its way into the stag's shoulder. Those days were gone, but still his interest in shooting was unabated.

Nothing had been altered on the place since he was a boy: the rent even was the same. But all that is now changed – swept away before modern improvements; and the rare old man is gone too, and I think his only enemy also.

There was nothing I used to look forward to, as the summer waned, with so much delight as the snipe shooting. Regularly as the swallow to the eaves in spring, the snipe comes back with the early frosts of autumn to the same well-known spots – to the bend of the brook or the boggy corner in the ploughed field – but in most uncertain numbers. Sometimes flocks of ten or twenty, sometimes only twos and threes are seen, but always haunting particular places.

They have a special affection for peaty ground, black and spongy, where every footstep seems to squeeze water out of the soil with a slight hissing sound, and the boot cuts through the soft turf. There, where a slow stream winds in and out, unmarked by willow or bush, but fringed with green aquatic grasses growing on a margin of ooze, the snipe finds tempting food; or in the meadows where a little spring breaks forth in the ditch and does not freeze – for water which has just bubbled out of the earth possesses this peculiarity, and is therefore favourable to low forms of insect or slug life in winter – the snipe may be found when the ponds are bound with ice.

Some of the old country folk used to make as much mystery about this bird as the cuckoo. Because it was seldom seen till the first fogs the belief was that it had lost its way in the mist at sea, and come inland by mistake.

Just as in the early part of the year green buds and

opening flowers welcome swallow and cuckoo, so the colours of the dying leaf prepare the way for the second feathered immigration in autumn. Once now and then the tints of autumn are so beautiful that the artist can hardly convey what he sees to canvas. The maples are aglow with orange, the oaks one mass of buff, the limes light gold, the elms a soft yellow. In the hawthorn thickets bronze spots abound; here and there a bramble leaf has turned a brilliant crimson (though many bramble leaves will remain a dull green all the winter through); the edible chestnut sheds leaves of a dark fawn hue, but all, scattered by the winds, presently resolve into a black pulp upon the earth. Noting these signs the sportsman gets out his dust-shot for the snipe, and the farmer, as he sees the fieldfare flying over after a voyage from Norway, congratulates himself that last month was reasonably dry, and enabled him to sow his winter seed.

'Sceap – sceap!' and very often the snipe successfully carries out the intention expressed in his odd-sounding cry, and does escape in reality. Although I could not at first put my theory into practice, yet I found by experience that it was correct. He is the exception to the golden rule that the safest way lies in the middle, and that therefore you should fire not too soon nor too late, but half-way between. But the snipe must either be knocked over the instant he rises from the ground, and before he has time to commence his puzzling zig-zag flight, or else you must wait till he has finished his corkscrew burst.

Then there is a moment just before he passes out of range when he glides in a straight line and may be hit. This singular zig-zag flight so deceives the eye as almost to produce the idea of a spiral movement. No barrel can ever be jerked from side to side swiftly enough, no hair-trigger is fine enough, to catch him then, except by the chance of a vast scattering over-charge, which has nothing to do with sport. If he rises at some little distance, then fire instantly, because by the time the zig-zag is done the range will be too great; if he starts up under your feet, out of a bunch of rushes, as is often the case, then give him law till his eccentric twist is finished.

When the smoke has cleared away in the crisp air, there he lies, the yet warm breast on the frozen ground, to be lifted up not without a passing pity and admiration. The brown feathers are exquisitely shaded, and so exactly resemble the hue of the rough dead aquatic grass out of which he sprang that if you cast the bird among it you will have some trouble to find it again. To discover a living snipe on the ground is indeed a test of good eye-sight; for as he slips in and out among the brown withered flags and the grey grass it requires not only a quick eye but the inbred sportsman's instinct of perception (if such a phrase is permissible) to mark him out.

If your shot has missed and merely splashed up the water or rattled against bare branches, then step swiftly behind a tree-trunk, and stay in ambuscade, keeping a sharp watch on him as he circles round high up in the air. Very often in a few minutes he will come back in a wide sweep, and drop scarcely a gun-shot distant in the same watercourse, when a second shot may be obtained. The little jack snipe, when flushed, will never fly far, if shot at several times in succession, still settling fifty or sixty yards farther on, and is easily bagged.

Coming silently as possible round a corner, treading gently on the grass still white with hoar-frost in the shadow of the bushes, you may chance to spring a stray woodcock, which bird, if you lose a moment, will put the hedge between him and you. Artists used to seek for certain feathers which he carries, one in each wing, thinking to make of them a more delicate brush than the finest camel's hair.

In the evening I used to hide in the osier-beds on the edge of a great water-meadow; for now that the marshes are drained, and the black earth of the fens yields a harvest of yellow corn, the broad level meads which are irrigated to fertilise them are among the chief inland resorts of wildfowl. When the bright moon is rising, you walk in among the tapering osier-wands, the rustling sedges, and dead dry hemlock stems, and wait behind an aspen tree.

In the thick blackthorn bush a round dark ball indicates the blackbird, who has puffed out his feathers to shield him from the frost, and who will sit so close and quiet that you may see the moonlight glitter on his eye. Presently comes a whistling noise of wings, and a loud 'quack, quack!' as a string of ducks, their long necks stretched out, pass over not twenty yards high, slowly slanting downwards to the water. This is the favourable moment for the gun, because their big bodies are well defined against the sky, and aim can be taken; but to shoot anything on the ground at night, even a rabbit, whose white tail as he hops away is fairly visible, is most difficult.

The baffling shadows and the moonbeams on the

barrel, and the faint reflection from the dew or hoar-frost on the grass, prevent more than a general direction being given to the gun, even with the tiny piece of white paper which some affix to the muzzle-sight as a guide. From a punt with a swivel gun it is different, because the game is swimming and visible as black dots on the surface, and half a pound of shot is sure to hit something. But in the water-meadows the ducks get among the grass, and the larger water-carriers where they can swim usually have small raised banks, so that at a distance only the heads of the birds appear above them.

So that the best time to shoot a duck is just as he slopes down to settle – first, because he is distinctly visible against the sky; next, because he is within easy range; and lastly, his flight is steady. If you attempt to have ducks driven towards you, though they may go right overhead, yet it will often be too high – for they rise at a sharp angle when frightened; and men who are excellent judges of distance when it is a hare running across the fallow, find themselves all at fault trying to shoot at any elevation. Perhaps this arises from the peculiarity of the human eye which draughtsmen are fond of illustrating by asking a tyro to correctly bisect a vertical line: a thing that looks easy, and is really only to be done by long practice.

To make certain of selecting the right spot in the osiers over which the ducks will pass, for one or two evenings previously a look-out should be kept and their usual course observed; for all birds and animals, even the wildest wildfowl, are creatures of habit and custom, and having once followed a particular path will continue to use it until seriously disturbed. Evening after evening the ducks will rise above the horizon at the same place and almost at the same time, and fly straight to their favourite feeding place.

If hit, the mallard falls with a thud on the earth, for he is a heavy bird; and few are more worthy of powder and shot either for his savoury flavour, far surpassing the tame duck, or the beauty of his burnished neck. With the ducks come teal and widgeon and moorhen, till the swampy meadow resounds with their strange cries. When ponds and lakes are frozen hard is the best time for sport in these irrigated fields. All day long the ducks will stand or waddle to and fro on the ice in the centre of the lake or mere, far out of reach and ready to rise at the slightest alarm. But at night they seek the meadow where the water, running swiftly in the carriers, never entirely freezes, and where, if the shallow spots become ice, the rising current flows over it and floods another place.

There is, moreover, never any difficulty in getting the game when hit, because the water, except in the main carriers, which you can leap across, hardly rises to the ankle, and ordinary water-tight boots will enable you to wade wherever necessary. This is a great advantage with wildfowl, which are sometimes shot and lost in deep ooze and strong currents and eddies, and on thin ice where men cannot go and even good dogs are puzzled.

5. Ferreting: A Rabbit-Hunter

The ferreting season commences when the frosts have caused the leaves to drop, and the rabbits grow fat from feeding on bark. Early one December morning, Orion and I started, with our man Little John, to ferret a double-mound for our old friend Farmer 'Willum' at Redcote.

Little John was a labourer – one of those frequently working at odd times for Luke, the Rabbit-Contractor. We had nicknamed him Little John because of his great size and unwieldy proportions. He was the most useful man we knew for such work; his heart was so thoroughly in it.

He was waiting for us before we had finished breakfast, with his tools and implements, having carefully prepared these while yet it was dark at home in his cottage. The nets require looking to before starting, as they are apt to get into a tangle, and there is nothing so annoying as to have to unravel strings with chilled fingers in a ditch. Some have to be mended, having been torn; some are cast aside altogether because weak and rotten. The twine having been frequently saturated with water has decayed. All the nets are of a light yellow colour from the clay and sand that has worked into the string.

These nets almost filled a sack, into which he also cast a pair of 'owl-catchers', gloves of stout white leather, thick enough to turn a thorn while handling bushes, or to withstand the claws of an owl furiously resisting capture. His ferrets cost him much thought, which to take and which to leave behind. He had also to be particular how he fed them – they must be eager for prey, and yet they must not be starved, else they would gorge on the blood of the first rabbit, and become useless for hunting.

Two had to be muzzled – an operation of some difficulty that generally results in a scratched hand. A small piece of small but strong twine is passed through the jaws behind the tusk-like teeth, and tightly tied round, so tightly as almost to cut into the skin. This is the old way of muzzling a ferret, handed down from generations: Little John scorns the muzzles that can be bought at shops, and still more despises the tiny bells to hang round the neck. The first he says often come off, and the second embarrass the ferret and sometimes catch in projecting rootlets and hold it fast. He has, too, a line – many yards of stout twine wound about a short stick – to line a ferret if necessary.

The ferrets are placed in a smaller bag, tightly tied at the top – for they will work through and get out if any aperture be left. Inside the bag is a little hay for them to lay on. He prefers the fitchew ferret as he calls it; that is the sort that are coloured like a polecat. He says they are fiercer, larger of make and more powerful. But he has also a couple of white ones with pink eyes. Besides the sack of nets, the bag of ferrets, and a small bundle in a knotted handkerchief – his 'nuncheon' – which in themselves make a tolerable load, he has brought a billhook, and a 'navigator', or draining-tool.

This is a narrow spade of specially stout make; the blade is hollow and resembles an exaggerated gouge, and the advantage is that in digging out a rabbit the tool is very apt to catch under a root, when an ordinary spade may bend and become useless. The 'navigator' will stand anything, and being narrow is also more handy. All these implements Little John has prepared by the dim light of a horn lantern in the shed at the back of his cottage. A mug of ale while we get our guns greatly cheers him, and unlooses his tongue.

All the way to Redcote he impresses on us the absolute necessity of silence while ferreting, and congratulates us on having a nearly still day. He is a little doubtful about Orion's spaniel and whether it will keep quiet or not.

When we reach the double-mound, his talk entirely ceases: he is as silent and as rugged as a pollard oak. By the top of the mound the sack of nets is thrown down on the sward and opened. As there are more holes on the other side of the hedge Orion goes over with Little John, and I proceed to set up the nets on mine.

I found some difficulty in getting at the bank, the bushes being so thick, and had to use the billhook and chop a way in: I heard Little John growling about this in a whisper to Orion. Very often before going with the ferrets, people send a man or two a few hours previously to chop and clear the bushes. The effect is that the rabbits will not bolt freely. They hear the men chopping, and the vibration of the earth as they clumsily climb over the banks, and will not come out till absolutely forced. If it is done at all, it should be done a week beforehand.

That was why Little John grumbled at my chopping though he knew it was necessary.

To set up a rabbit net you must arrange it so that it covers the whole of the mouth of the hole, for if there is any opening between it and the bank the rabbit will slip through. He will not face the net unless obliged to. Along the upper part, if the bank is steep, so that the net will not lie on it of itself, two or three little twigs should be thrust through the meshes into the earth to suspend it.

These twigs should be no larger than are used by birds in constructing their nests; just strong enough to hold the net in place and no more. On the other hand, care must be taken that no stout projecting root catches a corner of the net, else it will not draw up properly and the rabbit will escape.

Little John, not satisfied with my assurance that I had netted all the holes my side, now came over – crawling on hands and knees that he might not jar the bank – to examine for himself. His practised eye detected two holes that I had missed: one on the top of the mound much overhung by dead grass, and one under a stole. These he attended to. He then crawled up on the mound two or three yards below the end of the bury, and with his own hands stretched a larger net right across the top of the bank, so that if a rabbit did escape he would run into this. To be still more sure he stretched another similar net across the whole width of the mound at the other end of the bury.

He then undid the mouth of the ferret-bag, holding it between his knees – the ferrets immediately attempted to struggle out: he selected two and then tied it up again.

With both these in his own hands, for he would trust nothing to another, he slipped quietly back to Orion's side, and so soon as he saw I was standing well back placed them in different holes.

Almost the next instant one came out my side disarranging a net. I got into the ditch, hastily reset the net, and put the ferret to an adjacent hole, lifting up the corner of the net there for it to creep in. Unlike the weasel, a ferret once outside a hole seems at a loss, and wanders slowly about, till chance brings him to a second. The weasel used to hunting is no sooner out of one hole than he darts away to the next. But this power the ferret has partially lost from confinement.

For a moment the ferret hesitated inside the hole, as if undecided which of two passages to take: then he started, and I lost sight of his tail. Hardly had I got back to my stand than I heard Little John leap into the ditch his side: the next minute I saw the body of the rabbit which he had killed thrown out into the field.

I stood behind a somewhat advanced bush that came out into the meadow like a buttress, and kept an eye on the holes along the bank. It is essential to stand well back from the holes, and, if possible, out of sight. In a few moments something moved, and I saw the head of a rabbit at the mouth of a hole just behind the net. He looked through the meshes as through a lattice, and I could see his nostrils work, as he considered within himself how to pass this thing. It was but for a moment; the ferret came behind, and wild with hereditary fear, the rabbit leaped into the net.

The force of the spring not only drew the net together,

but dragged out the peg, and rabbit and net inextricably entangled rolled down the bank to the bottom of the ditch. I jumped into the ditch and seized the net; when there came a hoarse whisper: 'Look sharp you, measter: put up another net fust – *he* can't get out; hould un under your arm, *or in your teeth.*'

I looked up, and saw Little John's face peering over the mound. He had thrust himself up under the bushes; his hat was off; his weather-beaten face bleeding from a briar, but he could not feel the scratch so anxious was he that nothing should escape. I pulled another net from my pocket, and spread it roughly over the hole; then more slowly took the rabbit from the other net.

You should never hold a rabbit up till you have got fast hold of his hind legs; he will so twist and work himself as to get free from any other grasp. But when held by the hind legs and lifted from the ground he can do nothing. I now returned to my buttress of bushes and waited. The rabbits did not bolt my side again for a while. Every now and then I saw, or heard, Orion or Little John leap into their ditch, and well knew what it meant before the dead rabbit was cast out to fall with a helpless thud upon the sward.

Once I saw a rabbit's head at the mouth of a hole, and momentarily expected him to dart forth driven by the same panic fear. But either the ferret passed, or there was another side-tunnel – the rabbit went back. Some few minutes afterwards Little John exclaimed: 'Look out, you; ferret's out!' One of the ferrets had come out of a hole and was aimlessly – as it appeared – roaming along the bank.

As he came nearest my side, I got quietly into the ditch and seized him, and put him into a hole. To my surprise he refused to go in – I pushed him: he returned and continued to try to come out till I gave him a sharp fillip with the finger, when he shook the dust and particles of dry earth from his fur with a shiver, as if in protest, and slowly disappeared inside the hole.

As I was creeping out of the deep ditch on hands and knees, I heard Orion call angrily to the spaniel to come to heel. Hitherto the spaniel had sat on his haunches behind Orion fairly quiet and still, though not without an occasional restless movement. But now he broke suddenly from all control, and disregarding Orion's anger – though with hanging tail – rushed into the hedge, and along the top of the mound where there was a thick mass of dead grass. Little John hurled a clod of clay at him, but before I was quite out of the ditch the spaniel gave tongue, and at the same moment I saw a rabbit come from the ditch and run like mad across the field.

The dog gave chase – I rushed for my gun, which was some yards off, placed against a hollow withy tree. The haste disconcerted the aim – the rabbit too was almost fifty yards away when I fired. But the shot broke one hind leg – it trailed behind – and the spaniel had him instantly. 'Look at yer nets,' said Little John in a tone of suppressed indignation, for he disliked the noise of a gun, as all other noises.

I did look, and found that one net had been partly pushed aside; yet to so small an extent that I should hardly have believed it possible for the rabbit to have crept through. He must have slipped out without the slightest sound and quietly got on the top of the mound without being seen. But there, alas! he found a wide net stretched right across the bank so that to slip down the mound on the top was impossible. This would certainly have been his course had not the net been there.

It was now doubtless that the spaniel caught wind of him, and the scent was so strong that it overcame his obedience. The moment the dog got on the bank, the rabbit slipped down into the rushes in the ditch – I did not see him because my back was turned in the act to scramble out. Then, directly the spaniel gave tongue the rabbit darted for the open, hoping to reach the buries in the hedge on the opposite side of the meadow.

This incident explained why the ferret seemed so loth to go back into the hole. He had crept out some few moments behind the rabbit and in his aimless uncertain manner was trying to follow the scent along the bank. He did not like being compelled to give up this scent and to search again for another. 'Us must be main careful how us fixes our nets, you,' said Little John, going as far as he could in reproof of my negligence.

The noise of the gun, the barking, and talking was of course heard by the rabbits still in the bury, and as if to show that Little John was right, for a while they ceased to bolt. Standing behind the bushes – against which I now placed the gun to be nearer at hand – I watched the nets till my eye was caught by the motions of the ferret-bag. It lay on the grass and had hitherto been inert. But now the bag reared itself up, and then rolled over, to again rise and again tumble. The ferrets left in it in reserve were eager to get out – sharp set on account of a scanty breakfast – and their motions caused the bag to roll along a short distance.

I could see Orion on the other side of the mound tolerably well because he was standing up and the leaves had fallen from the upper part of the bushes. Little John was crouched in the ditch: the dead grasses, 'gicks,' withered vines of bryony, the thistles, and dark shrivelled fern concealed him.

There was a round black sloe on the blackthorn beside me, the beautiful gloss, or bloom, on it made it look like a tiny plum. It tasted not only sour, but seemed to positively fill the mouth with a rough acid. Overhead light grey clouds, closely packed but not rainy, drifted very slowly before a N. E. upper current. Occasionally a brief puff of wind came through the bushes rustling the dead leaves that still remained on the oaks.

Despite the cold, something of Little John's intense concentration communicated itself to us: we waited and watched with eager patience. After a while he got out of the ditch where he had been listening with his ear close against the bank, and asked me to pass him the ferret-bag. He took out another ferret and lined it – that is, attached one end of a long string to its neck, and then sent it in.

He watched which way the ferret turned, and then again placed his head upon the hard clay to listen. Orion had to come and hold the line, while he went two or three yards farther down, got into the ditch and once more listened carefully. 'He be about the middle of the mound you,' he said to me; he be between you and I. 'Lor! look out.'

There was a low rumbling sound – I expected to see

a rabbit bolt into one of my nets, I heard Little John moving some leaves, and then he shouted, 'Give I a net, you – quick. Lor! here be another hole: he's coming!' I looked over the mound and saw Little John, his teeth set and staring at a hole which had no net, his great hands open ready to pounce instantly like some wild animal on its prey. In an instant the rabbit bolted – he clutched it and clasped it tight to his chest. There was a moment of struggling, the next the rabbit was held up for a moment and then cast across his knee.

It was always a sight to see Little John's keen delight in 'wristing' their necks. He affected utter unconscious-ness of what he was doing, looked you in the face, and spoke about some indifferent subject. But all the while he was feeling the rabbit's muscles stretch before the terrible grasp of his hands, and an expression of com-placent satisfaction flitted over his features as the neck gave with a sudden looseness, and in a moment what had been a living straining creature became limp.

The ferret came out after the rabbit; he immediately caught it and thrust it into his pocket. There were still two ferrets in – one that was suspected to be gorging on a rabbit in a *cul de sac*, and the other lined, and which had gone to join that sanguinary feast. The use of the line was to trace where the loose ferret lay. 'Chuck I the show'l, measter,' said Little John.

I gave the 'navigator' tool a heave over the hedge; it fell and stuck upright in the sward. Orion handed it to him. He first filled up the hole from which a rabbit had just bolted with a couple of 'spits', *i.e.* spadefuls, and then began to dig on the top of the mound.

This digging was very tedious. The roots of the thorn bushes and trees constantly impeded it, and had to be cut. Then upon at last getting down to the hole, it was found that the right place had not been hit by several feet. Here was the line and the lined ferret – he had got hitched in a projecting root, and was furiously struggling to go forward to the feast of blood.

Another spell of digging – this time still slower because Little John was afraid lest the edge of his tool should suddenly slip through and cut his ferret on the head, and perhaps kill it. At last the place was reached and the ferret drawn forth still clinging to its victim. The rabbit was almost beyond recognition as a rabbit. The poor creature had been stopped by a *cul de sac*, and the ferret came upon him from behind.

As the hole was small the rabbit's body completely filled it, and the ferret could not scramble past to get at the spot behind the ear where it usually seizes. The ferret had therefore deliberately gnawn away the hindquarters and so bored a passage. The ferret being so gorged was useless for further hunting and was replaced in the bag. But Little John gave him a drink of water first from the bottom of the ditch.

Orion and I, wearied with the digging, now insisted on removing to the next bury, for we felt sure that the remaining rabbits in this one would not bolt. Little John had no choice but to comply, but he did so with much reluctance and many rueful glances back at the holes from which he took the nets. He was sure, he said, that there were at least half-a-dozen still in the bury: he only wished he might have all that he could get out of it. But we imperiously ordered a removal.

We went some thirty yards down the mound, passing many smaller buries, and chose a spot perfectly drilled with holes. While Little John was in the ditch putting up nets, we slily undid the ferret-bag and turned three ferrets at once loose into the holes. 'Lor! measter, measter, what be you at?' cried Little John, quite beside himself. 'You'll spoil all on it. Lor!'

A sharp report as Orion fired at a rabbit that bolted almost under Little John's fingers drowned his remonstrances, and he had to scramble out of the way quick. Bang! bang! right and left: the firing became rapid. There being no nets to alarm the rabbits and three ferrets hunting them, they tumbled out in all directions as fast as we could load. Now the cartridges struck branches and shattered them. Now the shot flattened itself against sarsen stones imbedded in the mound. The rabbits had scarce a yard to bolt from one hole to another, so that it was sharp work.

Little John now gave up all hope, and only pleaded piteously for his ferrets. 'Mind as you doan't hit 'em, measter; doant'ee shoot into a hole, you.' For half an hour we had some really good shooting: then it began to slacken, and we told him to catch his ferrets and go on to the next bury. I am not sure that he would not have rebelled outright but just then a boy came up carrying a basket of provisions, and a large earthenware jar with a bung cork, full of humming ale. Farmer Willum had sent this, and the strong liquor quite restored Little

John's good humour. It really was ale – such as is not to be got for money.

The boy said that he had seen Farmer Willum's hereditary enemy, the keeper, watching us from his side of the boundary, doubtless attracted by the sound of the firing. He said also that there was a pheasant in a little copse beside the brook. We sent him out again to reconnoitre: he returned and repeated that the keeper had gone, and that he thought he saw him enter the distant fir plantations. So we left the boy to help Little John at the next bury – a commission that made him grin with delight, and suited the other very well, since the noisy guns were going away, and he could use his nets.

We took the lined ferret with us, and started after the pheasant. Just as we approached the copse, the spaniel gave tongue on the other side of the hedge. Orion had tied him up to a bush, wishing to leave him with Little John. But the spaniel tore and twisted till he got loose and had followed us – keeping out of sight – till now crossing the scent of a rabbit he set up his bark. We called him to heel, and I am afraid he got a kick. But the pheasant was alarmed, and rose before we could properly enfilade the little copse, where we should most certainly have had him. He flew high and straight for the fir plantations, where it was useless to follow.

However, we leaped the brook and entered the keeper's territory under shelter of a thick double-mound. We slipped the lined ferret into a small bury, and succeeded in knocking over a couple of rabbits. The object of using the lined ferret was because we could easily recover it. This was pure mischief, for there were scores of rabbits on our own side. But then there was just a little spice of risk in this, and we knew Willum would gloat over it.

After firing these two shots we got back again as speedily as possible, and once more assisted Little John. We could not, however, quite resist the pleasure of shooting a rabbit occasionally and so tormenting him. We left one hole each side without a net, and insisted on the removal of the net that stretched across the top of the bank. This gave us a shot now and then, and the removal of the cross net allowed the rabbit some little law.

Notwithstanding these drawbacks – to him – Little John succeeded in making a good bag. He stayed till it was quite dark to dig out a ferret that had killed a rabbit in the hole. He took his money for his day's work with indifference: but when we presented him with two couple of clean rabbits his gratitude was too much for him to express. The gnawn and 'blown' rabbits [by shot] were his perquisite, the clean rabbits an unexpected gift. It was not their monetary value; it was the fact that they were rabbits.

The man's instinct for hunting was so strong that it seemed to overcome everything else. He would walk miles – after a long day's farm work – just to help old Luke, the rabbit contractor, bring home the rabbits in the evening from the Upper Woods. He worked regularly for one farmer, and did his work well: he was a sober man too as men go, that is he did not get drunk more than once a month. A strong man must drink now and then:

but he was not a sot, and took nine-tenths of his money faithfully home to his wife and children.

In the winter when farm work is not so pressing he was allowed a week off now and then, which he spent in ferreting for the farmers, and sometimes for Luke, and of course he was only too glad to get such an engagement as we gave him. Sometimes he made a good thing of his ferreting: sometimes when the weather was bad it was a failure. But although a few shillings were of consequence to him, it really did not seem to be the money-value but the sport that he loved. To him that sport was all-absorbing.

His ferrets were well looked after, and he sometimes sold one for a good price to keepers. As a rule a man who keeps ferrets is suspected: but Little John was too well understood, and he had no difficulty in begging a little milk for them.

His tenacity in pursuit of a rabbit was always a source of wonder to me. In rain, in wind, in frost; his feet up to the ankle in the ice-cold slush at the bottom of a ditch: no matter what the weather or how rough, he patiently stood to his nets. I have known him stand the whole day long in a snowstorm – the snow on the ground and in the holes, the flakes drifting against his face – and never once show impatience. All he disliked was wind – not on account of discomfort, but because the creaking of the branches and the howling of the blast made such a noise that it was impossible to tell where the rabbit would bolt.

He congratulated himself that evening because he had recovered all his ferrets. Sometimes one will lie in and defy all efforts to bring it out. One plan is to place a dead fresh rabbit at the mouth of the hole which may tempt the ferret to come and seize it. In large woods there are generally one or more ferrets wandering loose in the season, that have escaped from the keepers or poachers.

If the keeper sees one he tries to catch it; failing that, he puts a charge of shot into it. Some keepers think nothing of shooting their own ferrets if they will not come when called by the chirrup with the lips, or displease them in other ways. They do not care, because they can have as many as they like. Little John made pets of his: they obeyed him very well as a rule.

Poaching men are sometimes charged with stealing ferrets, i.e. with picking up and carrying off those that keepers have lost. A ferret is, however, a difficult thing to identify and swear to.

Those who go poaching with ferrets choose a moonlit night: if it is dark it is difficult to find the holes. Small buries are best because so much more easily managed, and the ferret is usually lined. If a large bury is attempted, they take the first half-dozen that bolt and then move on to another. The first rabbits come out rapidly; the rest linger as if warned by the fate of their companions. Instead of wasting time over them it is best to move to another place.

Unless a keeper should chance to pass up the hedgerow there is comparatively little risk, for the men are in the ditch and invisible ten yards away under the bushes and make no noise. It is more difficult to get home with the game: but it is managed. Very small buries with not more than four or five holes may be ferreted even on the darkest nights by carefully observing beforehand where the holes are situated.

6. Walks in the Wheat-fields

If you will look at a grain of wheat you will see that it seems folded up: it has crossed its arms and rolled itself up in a cloak, a fold of which forms a groove, and so gone to sleep. If you look at it some time, as people in the old enchanted days used to look into a mirror, or the magic ink, until they saw living figures therein, you can almost trace a miniature human being in the oval of the grain. It is narrow at the top, where the head would be, and broad across the shoulders, and narrow again down towards the feet; a tiny man or woman has wrapped itself round about with a garment and settled to slumber. Up in the far north, where the dead ice reigns, our arctic explorers used to roll themselves in a sleeping-bag like this, to keep the warmth in their bodies against the chilliness of the night. Down in the south, where the heated sands of Egypt never cool, there in the rock-hewn tombs lie the mummies wrapped and lapped and wound about with a hundred yards of linen, in the hope, it may be, that spices and balm might retain within the sarcophagus some small fragment of human organism through endless ages, till at last the gift of life revisited it. Like a grain of wheat the mummy is folded in its cloth. And I do not know really whether I might not say that these little grains of English corn do not hold within them the actual flesh and blood of man. Transubstantiation is a fact there.

Sometimes the grains are dry and shrivelled and hard as shot, sometimes they are large and full and have a juiciness about them, sometimes they are a little bit red, others are golden, many white. The sack stands open in the market – you can thrust your arm in it a foot deep, or take up a handful and let it run back like a liquid stream, or hold it in your palm and balance it, feeling the weight. They are not very heavy as they lie in the palm, yet these little grains are a ponderous weight that rules man's world. Wherever they are there is empire. Could imperial Rome have only grown sufficient wheat in Italy to have fed her legions Caesar would still be master of three-fourths of the earth. Rome thought more in her latter days of grapes and oysters and mullets, that change colour as they die, and singing girls and flute-playing, and cynic verse of Horace – anything rather than corn. Rome is no more, and the lords of the world are they who have mastership of wheat. We have the mastership at this hour by dint of our gold and our hundred-ton guns, but they are telling our farmers to cast aside their corn, and to grow tobacco and fruit and anything else that can be thought of in preference. The gold is slipping away. These sacks in the market open to all to thrust their hands in are not sacks of corn but of golden sovereigns, half-sovereigns, new George and the dragon, old George and the dragon, Sydney mint sovereigns, Napoleons, half Napoleons, Belgian gold, German gold, Italian gold; gold scraped and scratched and gathered together like old rags from door to door. Sacks full of gold, verily I may say that all the gold poured out from the Australian fields, every pennyweight of it, hundreds of tons, all shipped over the sea to India, Australia, South Africa, Egypt, and, above all, America, to buy wheat. It was said that Pompey and his sons covered the great earth with their bones, for each one died in a different quarter of the world; but now he would want two more sons for Australia and America, the two new quarters which are now at work ploughing, sowing, reaping, without a month's intermission, growing corn for us. When you buy a bag of flour at the baker's you pay fivepence over the counter, a very simple transaction. Still you do not expect to get even that little bag of flour for nothing, your fivepence goes over the counter in somebody else's till. Consider now the broad ocean as the counter and yourself to represent thirty-five millions of English people buying sixteen, seventeen, or eighteen million quarters of wheat from the nations opposite, and paying for it shiploads of gold.

So that these sacks of corn in the market are truly filled with gold dust; and how strange it seems at first that our farmers, who are for ever dabbling with their hands in these golden sands, should be for ever grumbling at their poverty! 'The nearer the church the farther from God' is an old country proverb; the nearer to wheat the farther from mammon, I may construct as an addendum. Quite lately a gentleman told me that while he grew wheat on his thousand acres he lost just a pound an acre per annum, i.e. a thousand a year out of capital, so that if he had not happily given up this amusement he would now have been in the workhouse munching the putty there supplied for bread.

The rag and bone men go from door to door filling

an old bag with scraps of linen, and so innumerable agents of bankers and financiers, vampires that suck gold, are for ever prowling about collecting every golden coin they can scent out and shipping it over sea. And what does not go abroad is in consequence of this great drain sharply locked up in the London safes as reserves against paper, and cannot be utilized in enterprises or manufacture. Therefore trade stands still, and factories are closed, and shipyards are idle, and beautiful vessels are stored up doing nothing by hundreds in dock; coal mines left to be filled with water, and furnaces blown out. Therefore there is bitter distress and starvation, and cries for relief works, and one meal a day for Board school children, and the red flag of Socialism is unfurled. All because of these little grains of wheat.

They talked of bringing artillery, with fevered lips, to roar forth shrapnel in Trafalgar Square; why not Gatling guns? The artillery did not come for very shame, but the Guards did, and there were regiments of infantry in the rear, with glittering bayonets to prod folk into moving on. All about these little grains of wheat.

These thoughts came into my mind in the winter afternoon at the edge of a level corn-field, with the copper-sheathed spire of the village church on my right, the sun going down on the left. The copper did not gleam, it was dull and brown, no better than discoloured wood, patched with pieces of later date and another shade of dulness. I wish they would glitter, some of these steeples or some of our roofs, and so light up the reddish brown of the elms and the grey lichened oaks. The very rooks are black, and the starlings and the wintry fieldfares and redwings have no colour at a distance. They say the metal roofs and domes gleam in Russia, and even in France, and why not in our rare sunshine? Once now and then you see a gilded weather-cock shine like a day-star as the sun goes down three miles away, over the dark brown field, where the plough has been going to and fro through the slow hours. I can see the plough and the horses very well at three miles, and know what they are doing.

I wish the trees, the elms, would grow tall enough and thick enough to hide the steeples and towers which stand up so stiff and stark, and bare and cold, some of them blunted and squab, some of them sharp enough to impale, with no more shape than a walking-stick, ferrule upwards – every one of them out of proportion and jarring to the eye. If by good fortune you can find a spot where you cannot see a steeple or a church tower, where you can see only fields and woods, you will find it so much more beautiful, for nature has made it of its kind perfect. The dim sea is always so beautiful a view because it is not disfigured by these buildings. In the ships men live; in the houses among the trees they live; these steeples and towers are empty, and no spirit can dwell in that which is out of proportion. Scarcely any one can paint a picture of the country without sticking in one of these repellent structures. The oast-houses, whose red cones are so plentiful in Kent and Sussex, have quite a different effect; they have some colour, and by a curious felicity the builders have hit upon a good proportion, so that the shape is pleasant; these, too, have some use in the world.

Westward the sun was going down over the sea, and a wild west wind, which the glow of the sun as it touched the waves seemed to heat into fury, brought up the distant sound of the billows from the beach. A line of dark Spanish oaks from which the sharp pointed acorns were dropping, darkest green oaks, shut out the shore. A thousand starlings were flung up into the air out of these oaks, as if an impatient hand had cast them into the sky; then down they fell again, with a ceaseless whistling and clucking; up they went and down they came, lost in the deep green foliage as if they had dropped in the sea. The long level of the wheat-field plain stretched out from my feet towards the far-away Downs, so level that the first hedge shut off the fields beyond; and every now and then over these hedges there rose up the white forms of sea-gulls drifting to and fro among the elms. White sea-gulls – birds of divination, you might say – a good symbol of the times, for now we plough the ocean. The barren sea! In the Greek poets you may find constant reference to it as that which could not be reaped or sowed. Ulysses, to betoken his madness, took his plough down to the shore and drew furrows in the sand – the sea that even Demeter, great goddess, could not sow nor bring to any fruition. Yet now the ocean is our wheat-field and ships are our barns. The sea-gull should be painted on the village tavern sign instead of the golden wheatsheaf.

There could be no more flat and uninteresting surface than this field, a damp wet brown, water slowly draining out of the furrows, not a bird that I can see. No hare certainly, or partridge, or even a rabbit – nothing to sit or crouch – on that cold surface, tame and level as the brown cover of a book. They like something more human and comfortable; just as we creep into nooks and corners of rooms and into cosy arm-chairs, so they like tufts or some growth of shelter, or mounds that are dry, between hedges where there is a bite for them. I can trace nothing on this surface, so heavily washed by late rain. Let now the harriers come, and instantly the hounds' second sense of smell picks up the invisible sign of the hare that has crossed it in the night or early dawn, and runs it as swiftly as if he were lifting a clue of thread. The dull surface is all written over with hieroglyphics to the hound, he can read and translate to us in joyous tongue. Or the foxhounds carry a bee-line straight from hedge to hedge, and after them come the hoofs, prospecting deeply into the earth, dashing down fibre and blade, crunching up the tender wheat and battering it to pieces. It will rise again all the fresher and stronger, for there is something human in wheat, and the more it is trampled on the better it grows. Despots grind half the human race, and despots stronger than man – plague, pestilence, and famine – grind the whole; and yet the world increases, and the green wheat of the human heart is not to be trampled out.

The starlings grew busier and busier in the dark green Spanish oaks, thrown up as if a shell had burst among them; suddenly their clucking and whistling ceased, the speeches of contention were over, a vote of confidence had been passed in their Government, and the House was silent. The pheasants in the park shook their wings and crowed 'kuck, kuck – kow', and went to roost; the water in the furrows ceased to reflect; the dark earth grew darker and damper; the elms lost their reddish brown; the sky became leaden behind the ridge of the Downs, and the shadow of night fell over the field.

Twenty-five years ago I went into a camera obscura, where you see miniature men and women, coloured photographs alive and moving, trees waving, now and then dogs crossing the bright sun picture. I was only there a few moments, and I have never been in one since, and yet so inexplicable a thing is memory, the picture stands before me now clear as if it were painted and tangible. So many millions of pictures have come and gone upon the retina, and yet I can single out this one in an instant, and take it down as you would a book from a shelf. The millions of coloured etchings that have fixed themselves there in the course of those years are all in due order in the portfolio of the mind, and yet they cannot occupy the space of a pin's point. They have neither length, breadth, nor thickness, none of the qualifications of mathematical substance, and yet they must in some way be a species of matter. The fact indicates the possibility of still more subtle existences. Now I wish I could put before you a coloured, living, moving picture, like that of the camera obscura, of some other wheat-fields at a sunnier time. They were painted on the surface of a plain, set round about with a margin of green downs. They were large enough to have the charm of vague, indefinite extension, and yet all could be distinctly seen. Large squares of green corn that was absorbing its yellow from the sunlight, chess squares, irregularly placed, of brown furrows; others of rich blood-red trifolium; others of scarlet sainfoin and blue lucerne, gardens of scarlet poppies here and there. Not all of these, of course, at once, but they followed so quickly in the summer days that they seemed to be one and the same pictures, and had you painted them altogether on the same canvas, together with ripe wheat, they would not have seemed out of place. Never was such brilliant colour; it was chalk there, and on chalk the colours are always clearer, the poppies deeper, the yellow mustard and charlock a keener yellow; the air, too, is pellucid. Waggons going along the tracks; men and women hoeing; ricks of last year still among clumps of trees, where the chimneys and gables of farmhouses are partly visible; red-tiled barns away yonder; a shepherd moving his hurdles; away again the black funnel of an idle engine, and the fly-wheel above hawthorn bushes – all so distinct and close under that you might almost fear to breathe for fear of dimming the mirror. The few white clouds sailing over seemed to belong to the fields on which their shadows were now foreshortened, now lengthened, as if they were really part of the fields, like the crops, and the azure sky so low down as to be the roof of the house and not at all a separate thing. And the sun a lamp that you might almost have pushed along his course faster with your hand; a loving and interesting sun that wanted the wheat to ripen, and stayed there in the slow-drawn arc of the summer day to lend a hand. Sun and sky and clouds close here and not across any planetary space, but working with us in the same field, shoulder to shoulder, with man. Then you might see the white doves yonder flutter up suddenly out of the trees by the farm, little flecks of white clouds themselves, and everywhere all throughout the plain an exquisite silence, a delicious repose, not one clang or harshness of sound to shatter the beauty of it. There you might stand on the high down among the thyme and watch it, hour after hour, and still no interruption; nothing to break it up. It was something like the broad folio of an ancient illuminated manuscript, in gold, gules, blue, green; with foliated scrolls and human figures, somewhat clumsy and thick, but quaintly drawn, and bold in their intense realism.

There was another wheat-field by the side of which I used to walk sometimes in the evenings, as the grains in the ears began to grow firm. The path ran for a mile beside it – a mile of wheat in one piece – all those million million stalks the same height, all with about the same number of grains in each ear, all ripening together. The hue of the surface travelled along as you approached; the tint of yellow shifted farther like the reflection of sunlight on water, but the surface was really much the same colour everywhere. It seemed a triumph of culture over such a space, such regularity, such perfection of myriads of plants springing in their true lines at the same time, each particular ear perfect, and a mile of it. Perfect work with the plough, the drill, the harrow in every detail, and yet such breadth. Let your hand touch the ears lightly as you walk – drawn through them as if over the side of a boat in water – feeling the golden heads. The sparrows fly out every now and then ahead; some of the birds like their corn as it hardens, and some while it is soft and full of milky sap. There are hares within, and many a brood of partridge chicks that cannot yet use their wings. Thick as the seed itself the feathered creatures have been among the wheat since it was sown. Finches more numerous than the berries on the hedges; sparrows like the finches multiplied by finches, linnets, rooks, like leaves on the trees, wood-pigeons whose crops are like bushel baskets for capacity; and now as it ripens the multitude will be multiplied by legions, and as it comes to the harvest there is a fresh crop of sparrows from the nests in the barns, you may see a brown cloud of them a hundred yards long. Besides which there were the rabbits that ate the young green blades, and the mice that will be busy in the sheaves, and the insects from spring-time to granary, a nameless host uncounted. A whole world, as it were, let loose upon the wheat, to eat, consume, and wither it, and yet it conquers the whole world. The great field you see was filled with gold corn four feet deep as a pitcher is filled with water to the brim. Of yore the rich man is said, in the Roman classic, to have measured his money, so here you might have measured it by the rood. The sunbeams sank deeper and deeper into the wheatears, layer upon layer of light, and the colour deepened by these daily strokes. There was no bulletin to tell the folk of its progress, no Nileometer to mark the rising flood of the wheat to its hour of overflow. Yet there went through the village a sense of expectation, and men said to each other, 'We shall be there soon.' No one knew the day – the last day of doom of the golden race; every one knew it was nigh. One evening there was a small square piece cut at one side, a little notch, and two shocks stood there in the twilight. Next day the village sent forth its army with their crooked weapons to cut and slay. It used to be an era, let me tell you, when a great farmer gave the signal to his reapers; not a man, woman, or child that did not talk of that. Well-to-do people stopped their vehicles and walked out into the new stubble. Ladies came, farmers, men of low degree, everybody – all to exchange a word or two with the workers. These were so terribly in earnest at the start they could scarcely acknowledge the presence even of the squire. They felt themselves so important, and were so full, and so intense and one-minded in their labour, that the great of the earth might come and go as sparrows for aught they cared. More men and more men were put on day by day, and women to bind the sheaves, till the vast field held the village, yet they seemed but a handful buried in the tunnels of the golden mine: they were lost in it like the hares, for as the wheat fell, the shocks rose behind them, low tents of corn. Your skin or mine could not have stood the scratching of the straw, which is stiff and sharp, and the burning of the sun, which blisters like red-hot iron. No one could stand the harvest-field as a reaper except he had been born and cradled in a cottage, and passed his childhood bare-headed in July heats and January snows. I was always fond of being out of doors, yet I used to wonder how these men and women could stand it, for the summer day is long, and they were there hours before I was up. The edge of the reap-hook had to be driven by force through the stout stalks like a sword, blow after blow, minute after minute, hour after hour; the back stooping, and the broad sun throwing his fiery rays from a full disc on the head and neck. I think some of them used to put handkerchiefs doubled up in their hats as pads, as in the East they wind the long roll of the turban about the head, and perhaps they would have done better if they had adopted the custom of the South and wound a long scarf about the middle of the body, for they were very liable to be struck down with such internal complaints as come from great heat. Their necks grew black, much like black oak in old houses. Their open chests were always bare, and flat, and stark, and never rising with rounded bust-like muscle as the Greek statues of athletes.

The breast-bone was burned black, and their arms, tough as ash, seemed cased in leather. They grew visibly thinner in the harvest-field, and shrunk together – all flesh disappearing, and nothing but sinew and muscle remaining. Never was such work. The wages were low in those days, and it is not long ago, either – I mean the all-year-round wages; the reaping was piecework at so much per acre – like solid gold to men and women who had lived on dry bones, as it were, through the winter. So they worked and slaved, and tore at the wheat as if they were seized with a frenzy; the heat, the aches, the illness, the sunstroke, always impending in the air – the stomach hungry again before the meal was over, it was nothing. No song, no laugh, no stay – on from morn till night, possessed with a maddened desire to labour, for the more they could cut the larger the sum they would receive; and what is man's heart and brain to money? So hard, you see, is the pressure of human life that these miserables would have prayed on their knees for permission to tear their arms from the socket, and to scorch and shrivel themselves to charred human brands in the furnace of the sun.

Does it not seem bitter that it should be so? Here was the wheat, the beauty of which I strive in vain to tell you, in the midst of the flowery summer, scourging them with the knot of necessity; that which should give life pulling the life out of them, rendering their existence below that of the cattle, so far as the pleasure of living goes. Without doubt many a low mound in the church-yard – once visible, now level – was the sooner raised over the nameless dead because of that terrible strain in the few weeks of the gold fever. This is human life, real human life – no rest, no calm enjoyment of the scene, no generous gift of food and wine lavishly offered by the gods – the hard fist of necessity for ever battering man to a shapeless and hopeless fall.

The whole village lived in the field; a corn-land village is always the most populous, and every rood of land thereabouts, in a sense, maintains its man. The reaping, and the binding up and stacking of the sheaves, and the carting and building of the ricks, and the gleaning, there was something to do for every one, from the 'olde, olde, very olde man', the Thomas Parr of the hamlet, down to the very youngest child whose little eye could see, and whose little hand could hold a stalk of wheat. The gleaners had a way of binding up the collected wheatstalks together so that a very large quantity was held tightly in a very small compass. The gleaner's sheaf looked like the knot of a girl's hair woven in and bound. It was a tradition of the wheat-field handed down from generation to generation, a thing you could not possibly do unless you had been shown the secret – like the knots the sailors tie, a kind of hand art. The wheatstalks being thick at one end makes the sheaf heavier and more solid there, and so in any manner of fastening it or stacking it, it takes a rounded shape like a nine-pin; the round ricks are built thick in the middle and lessen gradually toward the top and toward the ground. The warm yellow of the straw is very pleasant to look at on a winter's day under a grey sky; so, too, the straw looks nice and warm and comfortable, thrown down thickly in the yards for the roan cattle.

After the village has gone back to its home still the work of the wheat is not over; there is the thatching with straw of last year, which is bleached and contrasts with the yellow of the fresh-gathered crop. Next the threshing; and meantime the ploughs are at work, and very soon there is talk of seed-time.

I used to look with wonder when I was a boy at the endless length of wall and the enormous roof of a great tithe barn. The walls of Spanish convents, with little or no window to break the vast monotony, somewhat resemble it: the convent is a building, but does not look like a home; it is too big, too general. So this barn, with its few windows, seemed too immense to belong to any one man. The tithe barn has so completely dropped out of modern life that it may be well to briefly mention that its use was to hold the tenth sheaf from every wheat-field in the parish. The parson's tithe was the real actual tenth sheaf bodily taken from every field of corn in the district. A visible tenth, you see; a very solid thing. Imagine the vast heap they would have made, imagine the hundreds and hundreds of sacks of wheat they filled when they were threshed. I have often thought that it would per- haps be a good thing if this contribution of the real tenth could be brought back again for another purpose. If such a barn could be filled now, and its produce applied to the help of the poor and aged and injured of the village, we might get rid of that blot on our civilization – the workhouse. Mr Besant, in his late capital story, 'The Children of Gibeon', most truly pointed out that it was custom which rendered all men indifferent to the suffer- ings of their fellow-creatures. In the old Roman days men were crucified so often that it ceased even to be a show; the soldiers played at dice under the miserable wretches; the peasant women stepping by jested and laughed and sang. Almost in our own time dry skeletons creaked on gibbets at every cross-road:

> When for thirty shillings men were hung,
> And the thirst for blood grew stronger,
> Men's lives were valued then at a sheep's –
> Thank God that lasts no longer.

So strong is custom and tradition, and the habit of thought it weaves about us, that I have heard ancient and grave farmers, when the fact was mentioned with horror, hum, and ah! and handle their beards, and mutter that 'they didn't know as 'twas altogether such a bad thing as they was hung for sheep-stealing'. There were parsons then, as now, in every rural parish preaching and teaching something they called the Gospel. Why did they not rise as one man and denounce this ghastly iniquity, and demand its abolition? They did nothing of the sort; they enjoyed their pipes and grog very comfortably.

The gallows at the cross-roads is gone, but the work-house stands, and custom, cruel custom, that tyrant of the mind, has inured us (to use an old word) to its existence in our midst. Apart from any physical suffering, let us only consider the slow agony of the poor old reaper when he feels his lusty arm wither, and of the grey bowed wife as they feel themselves drifting like a ship ashore to that stony waiting-room. For it is a waiting-room till the grave receives them. Economically, too, the workhouse is a heavy loss and drag.

Could we, then, see the tithe barn filled again with golden wheat for this purpose of help to humanity, it might be a great and wonderful good. With this tenth to feed the starving and clothe the naked; with the tenth to give the little children a midday meal at the school – that would be natural and true. In the course of time, as the land laws lessen their grip, and the people take possession of the earth on which they stand, it is more than probable that something of this kind will really come about. It would be only simple justice after so many centuries – it takes so many hundreds of years to get even that.

'Workhouse, indeed!' I have heard the same ancient well-to-do greybeards ejaculate, 'workhouse! they ought to be very thankful they have got such a place to go to!'

All the village has been to the wheat-field with reaping-hooks, and waggons and horses, the whole strength of man has been employed upon it; little brown hands and large brown hands, blue eyes and dark eyes have been there searching about; all the intelligence of human beings has been brought to bear, and yet the stubble is not empty. Down there come again the ever-increasing clouds of sparrows; as a cloud rises here another cloud descends beyond it, a very mist and vapour as it were of wings. It makes one wonder to think where all the nests could have been; there could hardly have been enough eaves and barns for all these to have been bred in. Every one of the multitude has a keen pair of eyes and a hungry beak, and every single individual finds something to eat in the stubble. Something that was not provided for them, crumbs that have escaped from this broad table, and there they are every day for weeks together, still finding food. If you will consider the incredible number of little mouths, and the busy rate at which they ply them hour by hour, you may imagine what an immense number of grains of wheat must have escaped man's hand, for you must remember that every time they peck they take a whole grain. Down, too, come the grey-blue wood-pigeons and the wild turtle-doves. The singing linnets come in parties, the happy greenfinches, the streaked yellowhammers, as if any one had delicately painted them in separate streaks, and not with a wash of colour, the brown buntings, chaffinches – out they come from the hazel copses, where the nuts are dropping, and the hedge berries turning red, and every one finds something to his liking. There are the seeds of the charlock and the thistle, and a hundred other little seeds, insects, and minute atom-like foods it needs a bird's eye to know. They are never still, they sweep up into the hedges and line the boughs, calling and talking, and away again to another rood of stubble without any order or plan of search, just sowing themselves about like wind-blown seeds. Up and down the day through with a zest never failing. It is beautiful to listen to them and watch them, if any one will stay under an oak by the nut-tree boughs, where the dragon-flies shoot to and fro in the shade as if the direct rays of the sun would burn their delicate wings; they hunt chiefly in the shade. The linnets will suddenly sweep up into the boughs and converse sweetly over your head. The sunshine lingers and grows sweeter as the autumn gives tokens of its coming in the buff bryony leaf, and the acorn filling its cup. They are so happy, the birds, yet there are few to listen to them. I have often looked round and wondered that no one else was about hearkening to them. Altogether, perhaps, they lead safer lives in England than anywhere else. We do not shoot them; the fowlers do mischief, still they make but little impression; there are few birds of prey, and there is not that fearful blood-thirstiness that makes a tropical forest so terrible in fact, under its outward show of glowing colour. There, with cruel hawks and owls, and serpents, and beasts of prey, a bird's life is one long terror. They are ever on the watch here, but they are not so fearfully harassed, and are not certain as it were beforehand to be torn to pieces. The land is well cultivated, and the more the culture the more the food for them. Frost and snow are their greatest enemies, but even these do not often last a great while. It is a land of woods, and above all of hedges, which are much more favourable to birds than forests, so that they are better off in England than in other countries. From the sowing to the reaping, the wheat-field gives a constant dole like the monasteries of old, only here it is no crust, but a free and bountiful largess. Then the stubble must be broken up by the plough, and again there is a fresh helping for them. Brown partridge, and black rook, and yellowhammer, all hues and degrees, come to the wheat-field.

THE STORY OF PENGUIN CLASSICS

Before 1946 ...'Classics' are mainly the domain of academics and students, without readable editions for everyone else. This all changes when a little-known classicist, E. V. Rieu, presents Penguin founder Allen Lane with the translation of Homer's Odyssey that he has been working on and reading to his wife Nelly in his spare time.

1946 The Odyssey becomes the first Penguin Classic published, and promptly sells three million copies. Suddenly, classic books are no longer for the privileged few.

1950s Rieu, now series editor, turns to professional writers for the best modern, readable translations, including Dorothy L. Sayers's *Inferno* and Robert Graves's *The Twelve Caesars*, which revives the salacious original.

1960s 1961 sees the arrival of the Penguin Modern Classics, showcasing the best twentieth-century writers from around the world. Rieu retires in 1964, hailing the Penguin Classics list as 'the greatest educative force of the 20th century'.

1970s A new generation of translators arrives to swell the Penguin Classics ranks, and the list grows to encompass more philosophy, religion, science, history and politics.

1980s The Penguin American Library joins the Classics stable, with titles such as *The Last of the Mohicans* safeguarded. Penguin Classics now offers the most comprehensive library of world literature available.

1990s Penguin Popular Classics are launched, offering readers budget editions of the greatest works of literature. Penguin Audiobooks brings the classics to a listening audience for the first time, and in 1999 the launch of the Penguin Classics website takes them online to an ever larger global readership.

The 21st Century Penguin Classics are rejacketed for the first time in nearly twenty years. This world famous series now consists of more than 1,300 titles, making the widest range of the best books ever written available to millions – and constantly redefining the meaning of what makes a 'classic'.

The Odyssey continues ...

The best books ever written

PENGUIN (🐧) CLASSICS

SINCE 1946